# Foreign and Second Language Learning

CAMBRIDGE LANGUAGE TEACHING LIBRARY
A series of authoritative books on subjects of central importance for all language teachers.

In this series:

*Teaching the Spoken Language: an approach based on the analysis of conversational English* by Gillian Brown and George Yule

*A Foundation Course for Language Teachers* by Tom McArthur

*Communicating Naturally in a Second Language: theory and practice in language teaching* by Wilga M. Rivers

*Speaking in Many Tongues: essays in foreign language teaching* by Wilga M. Rivers

*Teaching and Learning Languages* by Earl W. Stevick

*Foreign and Second Language Learning: language-acquisition research and its implications for the classroom* by William T. Littlewood

# Foreign and Second Language Learning

Language-acquisition research
and its implications
for the classroom

*William T. Littlewood*

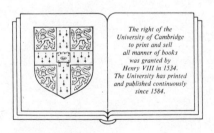

The right of the
University of Cambridge
to print and sell
all manner of books
was granted by
Henry VIII in 1534.
The University has printed
and published continuously
since 1584.

Cambridge University Press

Cambridge
London   New York   New Rochelle
Melbourne   Sydney

Published by the Press Syndicate of the University of Cambridge
The Pitt Building, Trumpington Street, Cambridge CB2 1RP
32 East 57th Street, New York, NY 10022, USA
296 Beaconsfield Parade, Middle Park, Melbourne 3206, Australia

First published 1984

Printed in Great Britain at The Pitman Press, Bath

Library of Congress catalogue card number: 83-23914

*British Library cataloguing in publication data*

Littlewood, William T.
   Foreign and second language learning.
   – (Cambridge language teaching library)
   1. Languages, Modern – Study and teaching
   I. Title
   418'.007'1      PB35

ISBN 0 521 25479 5   hard covers
ISBN 0 521 27486 9   paperback

# Contents

# Introduction

## About the book

This book is an introduction to some of the discoveries and ideas which have emerged from recent research into foreign and second language learning. In writing the book, I have tried to concentrate especially on those aspects which seem likely to help us develop more effective approaches to teaching.

The distinction between *teaching* and *learning* needs no explanation: the former is carried out by the teacher and the latter by the learner. It is surprising, then, that it is only comparatively recently – since the early 1970s – that the distinction has aroused much interest in language-teaching circles. In most of the considerable literature that exists about classroom methods and techniques, the focus of attention is clearly on the activity of teaching, as if learning were merely a straightforward reflection of the teacher's actions. 'To learn' means, above all, to react to stimuli and instructions provided by the main actor in the classroom: the teacher.

What, then, has led people to look more closely at the other participants in the teaching-and-learning process? It is not within the scope of this book to offer a detailed analysis of developments. However, I would mention the following factors as being particularly influential:

1  In almost every sphere of education, there has been a growing tendency to become more 'learner-centred'. We have come to realise that each person is ultimately responsible for his own learning and needs to engage his own personality in the educational process.
2  In language teaching, our methods and techniques have often failed to produce effective learning, however sound they may have appeared in theory. To discover why, we must study the learner.
3  Related to the previous point, we have become increasingly aware that individual learners are different from each other. They are not simply soft clay, waiting to be shaped by the teacher, but have their own personalities, motivations and learning styles. All of these characteristics affect how learners act in the classroom.
4  The active role which learners perform in developing their language has also been emphasised by studies of first language acquisition. These

have led to similar work in foreign and second language learning which, again, has shown the learner to be an active participant in the developmental process.

The content of the present book relates mainly to points 3 and 4 above: the nature of language development, the learner's role in it, and the factors which influence it. The aim of the book relates mainly to point 2: to examine aspects of learning which might help us improve teaching.

## Outline of the book

Chapter 1  discusses some of the studies and ideas about first language acquisition which have been influential in the field of second and foreign language learning.

Chapter 2  examines the habit-formation theories which were often dominant before this influence was felt.

Chapter 3  discusses learners' errors and what these might tell us about the internal processes which produce learning.

Chapter 4  looks at evidence that these processes dispose learners to master a language in predetermined sequences, which may conflict with our teaching sequences.

Chapter 5  considers why some people learn more successfully than others.

Chapter 6  tries to integrate some of the conclusions of previous chapters into a coherent picture of the learning experience.

Chapter 7  looks at some studies of how learners make use of a second or foreign language in order to communicate.

Chapter 8  suggests some ways in which recent evidence and ideas about learning may influence our approach to teaching.

At the end of the book, there are suggestions for further reading about many of the topics discussed in the book.

## How some terms are used in the book

A distinction is often made between 'foreign' and 'second' language learning. Briefly, a 'second' language has social functions within the community where it is learnt (e.g. as a lingua franca or as the language of another social group), whereas a 'foreign' language is learnt primarily for contact outside one's own community. I agree that this is a useful distinction. However, I have not needed to maintain it during most of the discussion in this book, and have therefore used the term *second language* as a cover term for both 'foreign' and 'second' language.

Another distinction which is sometimes made is that between 'learning' and 'acquisition'. Learning refers to conscious processes for internalising a second language, whereas acquisition refers to subconscious processes. Again, I have not found it necessary to make the distinction systematically. In any case, our knowledge about what is conscious and what is subconscious in second language learning is too vague for us to use the distinction reliably. I have therefore decided to use *learning* as a cover term, except when the distinction is crucial to the immediate discussion. When discussing a child's *first* language, I have followed the common convention of using 'acquisition' more freely.

Some writers reserve the term 'learning strategy' for conscious efforts to internalise language, in contrast with subconscious 'learning processes'. For other writers, a learning strategy may be either conscious or unconscious. It is the second usage that I have followed in this book.

Finally, whenever I have needed to use a pronoun to refer to the nouns 'learner' and 'teacher', I have used 'he', 'him' or 'his'. This is purely a linguistic convention and does not imply that the person is more likely to be male than female.

# 1 First language acquisition

## 1.1 Introduction

Over the past two decades, research in first language acquisition has had an enormous influence on the study of second language learning, both at the theoretical and at the practical level.

At the theoretical level, researchers in first language acquisition have been working with exciting new ideas about language and the learning process. Concepts such as imitation and habit-formation have to a large extent been replaced by notions which emphasise the child's own creativity in constructing his knowledge of the language. These same ideas have stimulated researchers to view second language learning from a similar perspective and to seek out concrete evidence to support this view.

At the practical level, first language researchers have developed new techniques for collecting and analysing children's speech. These same techniques, together with others, have been used in the field of second language learning, to gather data and accumulate evidence about the sequences and processes that are involved.

With this narrowing of the gap between theories and methods in the two fields, it is not surprising that a recurrent theme has been to consider the similarities and differences between first and second language learning. Often, our increased knowledge of first language acquisition has served as a backcloth for perceiving and understanding new facts about second language learning. In addition, many researchers see their long-term goal as to produce a single 'theory of language acquisition', which would account for first and second language learning within one framework. After all, the two experiences are both manifestations of the general human capacity to learn and use language.

These are the main reasons, then, why the opening chapter in this book about second language learning is devoted to a survey of some recent work in *first* language learning.

## 1.2 First language acquisition and behaviourism

Before the 1960s, the study of child language was dominated mainly by the 'behaviourist' approach to language and learning. The best-known proponent of this approach was B. F. Skinner.

The title of one of Skinner's major books, *Verbal Behavior* (1957), captures the essence of the behaviourist approach to language. Language is not a mental phenomenon: it is behaviour. Like other forms of human behaviour, it is learnt by a process of habit-formation, in which the main components are:

1 The child *imitates* the sounds and patterns which he hears around him.
2 People recognise the child's attempts as being similar to the adult models and *reinforce* (reward) the sounds, by approval or some other desirable reaction.
3 In order to obtain more of these rewards, the child *repeats* the sounds and patterns, so that these become habits.
4 In this way the child's verbal behaviour is *conditioned* (or 'shaped') until the habits coincide with the adult models.

The habit-formation process is essentially the same as when a pigeon's behaviour is shaped, so that it pecks at the correct discs in order to obtain food.

Within this framework, the child's own utterances were not seen as possessing a system in their own right. They were seen as a faulty version of adult speech. The 'mistakes' were simply the result of imperfect learning: the process of habit-formation had not yet had time to run its full course.

## 1.3   Inadequacies of the behaviourist approach

The behaviourist view of first language acquisition was strongly challenged from the 1960s onwards, especially under the influence of Noam Chomsky's linguistic theories and cognitive psychology. These are some of the arguments which have convinced most researchers of the inadequacies of the behaviourist approach:

1 The basic view of language is no longer acceptable. Language is not merely 'verbal behaviour'. Underlying the actual behaviour that we observe, there is a complex system of rules. These enable speakers to create and understand an infinite number of sentences, most of which they have never encountered before.

   This creativity would not be possible if we had to rely on individual bits of learnt behaviour. It is only possible because we have internalised the underlying system of rules. The knowledge of these rules is our linguistic 'competence', which is different from the 'performance' that we can actually observe.
2 What children learn, then, is an abstract knowledge of rules (or 'competence'). However, this is not what they are exposed to: they are

exposed only to people's speech ('performance'). This process of extracting abstract knowledge from concrete examples cannot be explained by habit-formation.

3 Such an explanation becomes even less feasible if we consider that the rules are often reflected very indirectly in the actual surface structure of the speech. For example, the surface structure of *John is easy to please* looks identical to that of *John is eager to please*, yet their 'deep' structure is completely different: in the first, it is a question of other people pleasing John, whereas in the second, it is John himself who wants to do the pleasing. Such information about deep relationships could not be acquired simply by observing and imitating verbal behaviour.

4 The learning task is therefore a complex one. It is perhaps more complex than any other learning task that most human beings undertake. Yet it occurs at a very early age and with exceptional speed: by the age of between three and a half and five, normally-endowed children have internalised all the basic structures of their language. Again, this cannot be explained by habit-formation alone.

5 Although children are exposed to different actual speech, they arrive at the same underlying rules as other children in their community. The evidence also suggests that they pass through similar sequences in acquiring these rules. From the outset, children seem to be constructing their own rule-systems, which they gradually adapt in the direction of the adult system. This means that the child's language is not simply being shaped by external forces: it is being *creatively constructed* by the child as he interacts with those around him.

As we shall see later, this 'creative construction' hypothesis has also had considerable influence on people's theories about *second* language learning.

## 1.4 An innate language-learning capacity?

Factors such as those just discussed have led many people to believe that children are born with an innate capacity for acquiring language. To describe this capacity, the term 'Language Acquisition Device' (often shortened to LAD) was coined by researchers. Some characteristics of the LAD would be:

1 It is specific to the human species and never fails to operate in normal human beings, from infancy to about the age of eleven.

2 It gives children a means of processing the speech in the environment so that they can construct its underlying system.

3 To enable it to operate so quickly, it may already contain some of the 'universal' features which are found in all known languages, such as

the use of word order to signal meaning, or basic grammatical relationships like that between subject and object.

The actual term 'LAD' has now lost a lot of its currency, but few people would question the basic notion that children possess an innate ability to acquire language. The main debate now concerns the extent to which there is a specific capacity earmarked for language alone. The other view is that language acquisition can be explained in terms of the same cognitive capacity used by children in making sense of other aspects of their world. For example, their ability to discover the relationship between subject and object in grammar may originate in their more general ability to perceive the world in terms of the agents and objects of actions. The truth may, of course, lie in between: first language learning may be partly a result of general cognitive capacities and partly a result of specific language-processing mechanisms, such as those mentioned in section 1.7.2.

If there is a special language-learning capacity and if this capacity declines at about the age of twelve, this is obviously significant in helping to explain why second language learning (unlike first language learning) is often unsuccessful. If there is no such 'critical period' for language learning, however, the causes for failure must be sought elsewhere, perhaps in other psychological factors or in the nature of the learning situation. We will return to this subject in chapter 5.

## 1.5 The grammatical development of children

Since the 1960s, there have been a large number of studies which have examined children's language not from the perspective of the adult's system, but in terms of its own underlying system. They have shown how children develop their grammatical system until it corresponds, eventually, to that of the adult community.

In this section, I will outline some of the main stages in this development.

### 1.5.1 *Telegraphic speech*

The early speech of children is often described as 'telegraphic'. This is because it lacks inflections and many of the small 'function words', such as articles or prepositions. The earliest stage consists of one-word utterances. Here are some examples taken from a stage when children are already joining two words to form an utterance:

allgone sticky (after the child had washed her hands)
allgone outside (after closing the door)
more page (asking an adult to continue reading)
sweater chair (indicating where the sweater is)

It is clear that, because the utterances are so reduced, the situation plays an important role in conveying the meaning. The result is that the same two words might convey very different meanings in different situations. For example, one child was heard to say *mommy sock* on two occasions: when picking up her mother's sock and when her mother was dressing her. In the first instance, then, the relationship between the two words was one of possession (as in 'this is mommy's sock'), whereas in the second, it was one of agent and object (as in 'mommy is putting on my sock').

Even at this stage, we can see that children use the language creatively, since they use utterances which they can never have actually heard. Nor can it be claimed that the utterances are simply imperfect attempts to imitate what the child might have heard from adults: it is difficult to think of an adult sentence where *allgone* and *sticky* would occur in that order, and *allgone outside* is clearly the child's own creation. Like the adult, then, the child is already making use of an ability to combine items from a limited set, in order to communicate meanings.

Attempts to write 'grammars' for children's two-word utterances have generally tried to do so in terms of two main classes of word: a restricted 'pivot' class and a much larger 'open' class. However, these attempts have not managed to account for all the two-word utterances which children have been heard to produce. A more fruitful approach has been to focus on the meanings which the utterances convey. Lois Bloom (1970) found, for example, that sentences containing two nouns were used to express five kinds of relationship (the interpretations depended on her observation of the child in an actual situation):

1 conjunction (e.g. *cup glass*, c.f. 'cup and glass');
2 description (e.g. *party hat*, c.f. 'a party hat');
3 possession (e.g. *daddy hat*, c.f. 'daddy's hat');
4 location (e.g. *sweater chair*, indicating where the sweater is);
5 agent – object (e.g. *mommy book*, c.f. 'mommy is reading a book').

Similarly, Dan Slobin (1979) looked at the communicative functions performed by two-word utterances in the speech of children acquiring six different languages. He found seven main types of function:

1 locating or naming (e.g. *there book, Buch da*);
2 demanding or desiring (e.g. *more milk, mehr Milch*);
3 negating (e.g. *not hungry, Kaffee nein*);
4 describing an event or situation (e.g. *block fall, Puppe kommt*);
5 indicating possession (e.g. *my shoe, Mamas Hut*);
6 describing a person or thing (e.g. *pretty dress, Milch heiss*);
7 questioning (e.g. *where ball, wo Ball*).

Another well-known analysis of children's speech in terms of its communicative functions is that of Michael Halliday (1975). Halliday argues that language acquisition takes place because the child realises he can *do* certain things with language, and that he learns these different functions in a predictable order: first, the child uses language to get what he needs (the 'instrumental' function); next, he uses it to control other people's behaviour (the 'regulatory' function), and so on. Halliday's 'functional' approach to language and language learning has also had considerable influence in the field of foreign and second language teaching.

Work on the meanings and functions of children's speech has led many people to play down the role of a specific language-acquisition capacity in explaining the child's development. They prefer to account for it more in terms of the child's growing mental capacity and communicative needs. The universal features which are found in all languages are then seen as resulting from the common ways in which people think and interact – that is, from universal features of human *cognitive* and *social* development.

## 1.5.2   *The development of inflections and function words*

Telegraphic speech extends beyond the two-word stage. For example, as the child's processing capacity grows, we find longer utterances which are still telegraphic:

> Andrew want that.
> Cat stand up table.

At the same time, however, children are in the process of mastering inflections (such as the *s* which belongs on *want* and *stand* in the above examples) and function words (such as the articles *a* or *the* which are also omitted above). In the relevant studies, these small items are usually referred to as *morphemes*, even though in normal linguistic terminology, 'morpheme' is a much wider concept.

Roger Brown (1973) studied how three children acquired fourteen of these morphemes in their first language. His findings came to have a wide influence not only for studies in first language acquisition, but also in the field of second language learning.

Children do not master each morpheme suddenly, from one day to the next, but gradually, over a period of time. One problem is therefore to decide at what point a morpheme should be counted as 'acquired'. The criterion which Brown used is that a child should produce it on 90 per cent of the occasions when the adult grammar requires it (i.e. in 90 per cent of the so-called 'obligatory contexts'). Applying this criterion, Brown found that the fourteen morphemes were acquired in a sequence which was remarkably similar for the three children. The 'average' order, from which individual children deviated only insignificantly, was:

1 present progressive -*ing* (as in *she is running*)
2 preposition *on*
3 preposition *in*
4 plural -*s* (as in *two books*)
5 irregular past forms (as in *she went*)
6 possessive *'s* (as in *daddy's hat*)
7 uncontractible copula (e.g. *is* in *yes, she is*)
8 articles *the* and *a* (which were classified together)
9 regular past -*ed* (as in *she walked*)
10 regular third-person-singular -*s* (as in *she runs*)
11 irregular third-person-singular forms (e.g. *she has*)
12 uncontractible auxiliary *be* (as in *she was coming*)
13 contractible copula (as in *she's tired*)
14 contractible auxiliary *be* (as in *he's coming*).

Brown also calculated the relative frequency of these morphemes in the speech of the children's parents. He found that the order of frequency does not correlate with the order of acquisition, which therefore cannot be explained in simple habit-formation terms. This is further evidence, then, that the child is an active contributor to the acquisition process.

Brown's study was 'longitudinal'. This means that he studied the three children's performance over the actual period of time when they were mastering the morphemes. Two other researchers, Jill and Peter de Villiers (1973), studied the same morphemes in the speech of twenty-one children in a 'cross-sectional' study. That is, they studied the speech of the children at one point in time. They then examined how well the children performed with the morphemes and 'scored' each morpheme according to how accurately the children produced it. They found that the accuracy order which they obtained by this method was similar to the acquisition order which Brown had obtained.

The study by the de Villiers is usually taken as significant from two points of view: it seems to confirm Brown's findings about the acquisition order for morphemes; it seems to justify the assumption that the 'accuracy order' obtained from a cross-sectional study can be taken as the equivalent of the 'acquisition order' which a longitudinal study would have revealed. Neither of these points is necessarily true. For example, it is possible that accuracy order and acquisition order are two different notions, in which case the de Villiers' study could actually be taken as *contradicting* that of Brown. However, the second assumption in particular is a very convenient one to make, since a cross-sectional study requires less time to complete than a longitudinal one. We shall see in chapter 4, in fact, that most of the comparable studies in second language learning have been cross-sectional. At the same time, we shall also see that many researchers have criticised the assumption that such studies reveal an *acquisition* order.

Children's acquisition of verb inflections provides some particularly interesting evidence for their active contribution to the learning process. Before they master the regular past inflection (e.g. the ending on *she walked*), they produce a number of common irregular past forms, such as *went* and *came*. At this stage, these forms are simply individual words for the child, not the result of a productive rule for forming the past tense. Then comes a point where the child seems to regress: instead of the 'correct' forms, he produces deviant utterances such as *Where it goed?* and *It comed off*. At a deeper level, however, these forms are not a sign of regression, but of progress in the child's developing system. He has now mastered a rule for forming the past tense: the same rule that enables the adult to form *walked* from *walk* or *climbed* from *climb*. This rule leads the child to produce *goed* and *comed*. Only later will he learn that *go* and *come* are in fact exceptions to this rule.

We shall see in chapter 3 how in the second language context, too, extensive use has been made of learners' errors, as evidence for the active process of 'creative construction' through which they come to terms with the second language system.

### 1.5.3 *The development of 'transformations'*

At the same time as children are increasing their mastery of grammatical morphemes, they are also increasing their ability to carry out 'transformations' on the basic sentence structure, in order to produce more complex utterances. The development of negatives and interrogatives has attracted particular attention. For both of these structures, children seem to follow similar sequences of development.

Here is the sequence that has been observed for the acquisition of negatives:

1. At first, the negative element is not part of the structure of the sentence. It is simply attached to the beginning or end, as in:
   No singing song.
   No the sun shining.
2. At the second stage of development, the negative element is inserted into the sentence. Instead of *no* or *not*, children may use *don't* or *can't*, but they do not yet inflect these for different persons or tenses:
   I no want envelope.
   He no bite you.
   He don't want it.
3. Children begin to produce the appropriate part of *do*, *be* or the modal verbs, to suit the person or tense:
   You don't want some supper.
   Paul didn't laugh.
   I am not a doctor.

With interrogatives, too, children first produce sentences in which the internal structure of the sentence is not affected. In yes/no questions, they first use intonation:

See hole?

You can't fix it?

For 'wh-interrogatives', the question word is at first simply placed in front of the sentence:

Where daddy going?

Why you caught it?

Where my spoon goed?

Later, children master the use of inversion with the auxiliary *do*, as in the adult system.

The development of these transformations provides interesting evidence that grammatical development is partly a matter of growing 'competence' (in the sense of underlying knowledge) and partly a matter of increasing 'performance' capacity. Ursula Bellugi-Klima (1968) found the following progression in the child's ability to carry out more than one transformation in a single utterance:

1 At one stage, the child can *either* invert subject and verb *or* prepose a question word, but not do both. We thus find inversion in yes/no questions (e.g. *Can he ride a truck?*) but not in wh-questions (e.g. *Where I can put them?*).

2 Later, the child is able to combine both operations, so that we find wh-questions with inversion (e.g. *Why can he go out?*). However, it may still be beyond the child's capacity to carry out three operations, so that the inversion may not take place if the sentence is also negated (e.g. *Why he can't go out?*).

3 Eventually, this limitation goes and the child is able to perform all three operations in the same utterance – prepose a question word, invert and negate (as in *Why can't he go out?*).

The evidence is not sufficient, however, to determine whether all children pass through these same stages.

As with the morpheme studies discussed in the previous section, the work carried out on negatives and interrogatives has had considerable influence in the field of second language learning. As we shall see in chapter 4, similar studies have been carried out with second language learners; comparisons have been drawn between sequences in first and second language learning; and much discussion has been generated about the nature of the underlying processes.

## 1.6   Later development

Later linguistic development has been the subject of less intensive study than that of the early years. However, it is clear that the limitations on the child's performance become less restrictive and that he becomes able to perform operations of a more and more complex nature. As well as operations within a single clause, these include the joining of two or more clauses into a complex sentence. There is evidence that this latter development starts with clauses used as objects of the verb (e.g. *I think it's the wrong way*).

Some subtle grammatical distinctions may not be mastered much before the age of ten. One of these is the distinction mentioned earlier (section 1.3) between *John is eager to please* and *John is easy to please*. Another is the distinction between *John asked Bill to come* and *John promised Bill to come* (the person who is expected to come is Bill in the first sentence, but John in the second). Studies with second language learners suggest that they, too, acquire these distinctions comparatively late.

Equally important, the child develops increasing knowledge of the conventions for varying speech according to the social situation. Craig Lawson found that even at the age of two, children were able to choose different styles of speech for addressing peers, older children and adults (quoted in Ervin-Tripp, 1977). In a study by Claudia Mitchell-Kernan and Keith Kernan (1977), children of seven used a range of forms for making requests which was comparable to the range used by adults. They were also clearly aware of the social significance of the various forms.

Both the ability to produce complex language and the ability to use appropriate styles are domains in which development is likely to continue well into adult life, in response to the person's widening communicative needs.

## 1.7   Cognitive factors in first language acquisition

As I said earlier, one of the important areas of debate is how first language acquisition is related to cognitive factors. In this section, I will summarise two main ways in which they may be related.

### 1.7.1   *Language and concepts*

In the first place, language development is dependent on the concepts which children form about the world and the meanings which they feel stimulated to communicate. Thus, Dan Slobin (1979) showed how children in several communities use two-word utterances to express a similar range of meanings (c.f. section 1.5.1). There is also evidence from later stages of an intimate relationship between cognitive and linguistic development. For example, Richard Cromer (1974) found that the English perfect tense (*he has walked*, etc.) was not used before the age of four and a half, despite the fact that the form is frequent in parents' speech and consists only of simple elements which were well within the children's capacity. He examined other aspects of the children's speech and decided that the perfect tense did not appear until they had acquired the underlying concept of 'present relevance'.

As well as conceptual development leading to language development, it is likely that the influence also works in the other direction: for example, the fact that 'present relevance' is embodied in the perfect tense helps to stimulate the English-speaking child to form the concept. Similarly, a language which makes a distinction between 'alienable' and 'inalienable' possession (e.g. *my book* as opposed to *my arm*) will encourage its speakers to make a distinction of which an English speaker may never become aware.

The second language learner has normally formed his basic concepts about the world, so that there cannot be the same link between language and cognitive development. Nonetheless, the link between language and concepts remains of major importance, since the second language will sometimes require the learner to develop an awareness for new concepts and distinctions (e.g. for the two kinds of possession mentioned above, or the two kinds of knowing embodied in German *wissen* and *kennen*).

### 1.7.2 Language-learning mechanisms

There is a second way in which cognitive factors influence first language acquisition. We have seen how children create order in the language data they encounter. For example, they form rules and, in some cases, over-generalise these rules to contexts where they do not apply (resulting in errors such as *comed* or *mouses*). Here, cognitive factors are determining not what meanings the child perceives and expresses, but how he makes sense of the linguistic system itself.

Dan Slobin (1973) has looked at children's acquisition sequences and errors in various languages and suggested that the child has a number of 'operating principles' for making sense of language data. For example:
- 'Avoid exceptions.' This principle might account for the tendency to overgeneralise rules, mentioned above.
- 'Underlying meaning-relationships should be marked clearly.' This might explain why the passive is more difficult for children than the active: there seems to be a natural tendency to prefer the first noun in a sentence to be the agent and the second to be the object.
- 'The use of grammatical markers should make semantic sense.' This

would explain why children have difficulty with distinctions which do not correspond to differences in meaning, such as the distinctions between genders in German or French.

In other words, children seem to look initially for a system (a) which is rule-governed in a consistent way, (b) in which the clues to meaning are clearly displayed, and (c) where each item or distinction has a definite function in communicating meaning.

This search for operating principles is obviously relevant for second as well as first language learning. Indeed, it may even be possible to generalise the three principles above directly to the second language context. Here, too, learners overgeneralise rules (producing forms such as *comed* or *mouses*); they have difficulty when items of language do not correspond clearly to items of meaning (e.g. many complex verb phrases); and they make errors with distinctions which are not necessary for the normal communication of meanings (e.g. genders or many of the case-endings in, say, German).

## 1.8   The language environment of the child

In a behaviourist approach to language acquisition, the child's environment is seen as exerting a major influence. It provides both the models which the child imitates and the rewards which make learning take place. In a cognitive approach, on the other hand, interest is drawn more towards the child's internal processes. Nonetheless, we should not forget that it is the environment which stimulates these processes and provides the material on which they operate. We should also not forget that although it has been shown that habit-formation processes (such as imitation and reinforcement) are not *sufficient* to explain first language acquisition, this does not mean that they do not play any role at all.

There have been a number of observational studies of the language addressed to small children by mothers, other adults or older children. These studies have shown that this so-called 'caretaker speech' has a number of characteristics which distinguish it from typical speech between adults. For example:

1  It is generally spoken more slowly and distinctly.
2  It contains shorter utterances.
3  It is more grammatical, with fewer broken sentences or false starts.
4  It contains fewer complex sentences (e.g. with two clauses).
5  There is less variety of tenses.
6  The range of vocabulary is more limited.
7  There is more repetition.
8  The speech is more closely related to the 'here-and-now'.

Caretaker speech seems particularly well suited to helping the child to learn the rules and meanings of the language. It is clearer to perceive and simpler in structure; the child has time to become familiar with a limited range of language; and meaning is clarified by repetition and reference to the immediate situation. If this special kind of input is, indeed, an important factor in the learning process, it may provide us with clues as to the kind of input that is most likely to facilitate second language learning.

Simplification could also make caretaker speech more suitable as a model for imitation. However, the role of imitation in the acquisition process is not clear. It seems that when children imitate an utterance they have just heard, they usually change it so that it conforms to the grammar (i.e. creative rules) that they themselves are operating at the time. Studies also suggest that children are most likely to imitate patterns that they have just learnt and are in the process of mastering. These findings would suggest that imitation plays a secondary, consolidating role, with the primary role being played by more creative, rule-forming processes.

The role of imitation is also unresolved in second language learning, as we shall see later in chapter 4 (section 4.6).

## 1.9 Summary

In this chapter, we have surveyed some recent work in first language acquisition, as a preliminary to looking at second language learning. We have seen how the behaviourist emphasis on habit-formation has given way to a more mentally-oriented approach, which stresses the child's active contribution to the learning process. This process of 'creative construction' seems to lead children through similar stages of development. There also seems to be a fruitful interaction between the children's linguistic and cognitive development. Finally, we have seen how the language environment of the child seems particularly well adapted to help learning take place.

# 2 Behaviourism and second language learning

## 2.1 Introduction

We saw in the previous chapter that before the 1960s, the field of first language acquisition was dominated by behaviourist ideas. These emphasised learning through habit-formation, which was brought about by imitation, reinforcement and repetition of behaviour.

Until about the mid-1960s, the field of second language learning was dominated by the same ideas. There is now an additional complicating factor, however. Whereas the first language learner is a novice so far as language habits are concerned, the second language learner already possesses a set of habits: his native language. Some of these earlier habits will help the new learning task. Others will hinder it.

## 2.2 Transfer and interference

From the behaviourist perspective, when first language habits are helpful to acquiring second language habits, this is *positive transfer*. For the English person learning French, an example of this would be the normal subject-verb-object sequence in declarative sentences: the English pattern (e.g. *The dog eats the meat*) can be transferred directly into French (*Le chien mange la viande*), so far as word order is concerned. However, if we replace the object with a pronoun, this transfer is no longer possible. English retains the same order as before (*The dog eats it*), but French places the object before the verb (*Le chien la mange*). The first language habit will now hinder the learner in learning the new one: it will predispose him to say *Le chien mange la*. This is now a case of *negative transfer* or, in the most common terminology, *interference*. In this way, differences between the two languages lead to interference, which is the cause of learning difficulties and errors.

Within the behaviourist framework, then, second language learning consists above all in overcoming the differences between the first and second language systems. Robert Lado summed up the learner's problem in a well-known formulation: 'Those elements that are similar to his native language will be simple for him, and those elements that are different will be difficult' (1957, p. 2). This has strong implications for second language instruction:

1  We can compare the learner's first language with the second language he is trying to learn (an activity which is usually called 'contrastive analysis').
2  From the differences that emerge from this analysis, we can predict the language items that will cause difficulty and the errors that the learner will be prone to make (a belief which is usually called the 'contrastive analysis hypothesis').
3  We can use these predictions in deciding which items need to be given special treatment in the courses that we teach or the materials that we write.
4  For these items in particular, we can use intensive techniques such as repetition or drills, in order to overcome the interference and establish the necessary new habits (such techniques forming the basis of so-called 'audio-lingual' or 'audio-visual' courses).

## 2.3   Levels of difficulty in second language learning

There are, of course, varying degrees of difference between language items and therefore, according to this contrastive viewpoint, varying levels of difficulty. A number of writers have drawn up schemes for judging these various levels, in order to provide a systematic basis for predicting learning difficulty.

Probably the best known of these schemes is the one proposed by Robert Stockwell et al. (1965) in their contrastive study of English and Spanish. Their 'hierarchy of difficulty' is based primarily on comparing what linguistic choices the learner must make in (a) his native language and (b) the language he is learning.

Stockwell et al. distinguish three types of choice:

1  no choice at all;
2  optional choice;
3  obligatory choice.

In their scheme, the highest level of difficulty occurs when there is no choice at all in the learner's mother tongue but an obligatory choice in the second language. For example, the English learner of Spanish must make an obligatory choice between *ser* and *estar* in contexts where English offers no choice but *to be*. At the other end of the hierarchy, the lowest level of difficulty is when there is an obligatory choice in both languages (e.g. the marking of plural nouns with the plural ending).

In phonology, the various combinations of the three types of choice, in mother tongue and second language, produce eight levels of difficulty. In grammar, there are sixteen possible combinations, because the scheme takes account not only of whether the grammatical choices correspond, but also of whether the choices have the same meaning or function. For example: level 10 in the hierarchy is when a structural choice is obligatory in both languages, but with different functions. An instance of this is the verb ending -*s*. This ending is an obligatory choice in both English and Spanish, but it marks the third person in English (*he speaks*) and the second person in Spanish (*hablas*).

This kind of scheme is obviously complex to grasp and apply. Even so, it does not really capture the many types of difference that can exist between two languages. For example, it does not cater for *partial* correspondence between two structures, as between the perfect tense in French and English: sometimes, the meaning is the same, but sometimes it is different. To take a further example: when a learner has to make an obligatory choice between items in the second language, the scheme takes no account of the number or complexity of the factors which *determine* the correct choice.

The basic assumption that degrees of difference correspond to levels of difficulty is itself problematic. In practice, there will be some items in a second language which present greater difficulty than others, even though they belong theoretically to the same level of difference. For example, the mastery of the distinction between perfective and imperfective aspect in Spanish is a more complex matter than mastering the number agreement between subject and verb, yet the scheme described above would place them at the same level in terms of choices to be made. Also, the fact that a structure or sound has no equivalent in the learner's mother tongue does not necessarily mean that it will be more difficult to learn because of that. On the contrary, such an item may be easier to learn than one which is only slightly different from a corresponding item in the mother tongue, since it is often very subtle differences that produce confusion and interference (a fact which is recognised in the behaviourist theory of transfer).

In other words, 'difference' and 'difficulty' are not identical concepts. The former derives from linguistic description and the latter from psychological processes, and there is no reason to believe that they should correlate with each other in a reliable way.

## 2.4 Testing the predictions

The behaviourist approach claims that we can predict difficulties and errors by means of contrastive analysis. This claim can, of course, be tested by practical results.

In practice, the claim has not been strongly supported by the evidence.

Teachers have found that errors predicted by contrastive analysis have often not occurred, whereas many actual errors would not have been predicted. In one empirical study, Randal Whitman and Kenneth Jackson (1972) used four different contrastive analyses of English and Japanese, in order to predict the errors that would be made by Japanese learners of English. They compared these predictions with the errors actually made by the learners in a series of tests. Their conclusion was that, whichever analysis they used, contrastive analysis was of little use in predicting the items which proved difficult in their tests.

We should perhaps note here that the assumption that errors are reliable indicators of difficulty is another questionable assumption which underlies the discussions of contrastive analysis. It is also possible that the more difficult aspects of learning stimulate the learner to draw on extra resources and therefore to *avoid* making errors.

## 2.5 Habit-formation versus creative construction

Practical experience suggests, then, that many errors made by learners would not have been predicted by contrastive analysis. This suggests, in turn, that interference from the mother tongue is not the only source of error. In turn again, this conclusion would hit at the very foundations of the behaviourist approach to second language learning by making us question the unique role of habit-formation in the learning process.

Heidi Dulay and Marina Burt (1973, 1974a) have attacked the role of interference and habit-formation in second language learning. They recorded the English speech of 145 children, aged between five and eight, whose native language was Spanish. They then studied how the children performed with six structures which differ in English and Spanish. In particular, they were interested in the proportion of two kinds of error:

1 'Interference errors', e.g. *They have hunger*, on the pattern of Spanish *Ellos tienen hambre*. According to behaviourist theory and the contrastive analysis hypothesis, this kind of error ought to predominate.
2 'Developmental errors', which resemble the errors made by children who are learning English as their mother tongue, e.g. *They hungry*.

According to Dulay and Burt's analysis, only 3 per cent of the children's errors could be classified as interference errors. On the other hand, they classified 85 per cent as developmental errors. The other 12 per cent did not fall clearly into either category.

This study was directly inspired by studies in first language acquisition, such as those discussed in chapter 1. These studies had indicated that 'creative construction' seemed to be a more powerful process than habit-formation in first language acquisition. Dulay and Burt wanted to show that the same was true of second language learning. They therefore interpreted the low proportion of interference errors and high proportion of developmental errors as proof that:

1 The process of habit-formation is as inadequate for explaining second language learning as it is for first language learning.
2 Children learning a second language, like their first language counterparts, develop through a process of 'creative construction'.

Most other researchers have not found such a small proportion of errors due to the influence of the mother tongue. Typically, they have categorised between a third and a half of learners' errors as due to transfer from the first language. We should note, however, that it is not necessary to see transfer as inextricably linked to behaviourist theories of habit-formation. It can also be seen as part of a process of creative construction: the transfer of rules from the mother tongue may be one of the learner's active strategies for making sense of the second language data. We shall see examples of this in the next chapter.

## 2.6 Conclusion

On its own, then, the behaviourist theory of habit-formation cannot account for second language learning. There must be other processes at work. However, this does not mean that habit-formation plays no role at all. Indeed, as we shall see later in connection with 'prefabricated' patterns and formulas (chapter 4, section 4.6), imitation may be an important component of the learning process.

In discussing contrastive analysis, Ronald Wardhaugh (1970) proposed that we should distinguish a 'strong' claim from a 'weak' claim. The strong claim is that contrastive analysis can reliably *predict* difficulty and errors. As we have seen, this claim is not supported by the evidence. The weak claim is, however, generally considered to be more acceptable. This is that, after we have observed what errors learners actually make, contrastive analysis can help to *explain* some of these errors, namely, those which are due to transfer. In this capacity, contrastive analysis becomes part of the wider undertaking of *error analysis*.

We will turn to error analysis in the next chapter.

# 3 Errors and learning strategies

## 3.1 Introduction

We saw in chapter 1 how, in studies of first language acquisition, attitudes have changed since the 1950s. A child's speech is no longer seen as just a faulty version of the adult's. It is recognised as having its own underlying system which can be described in its own terms. As the system develops towards that of the adult, the child contributes by actively forming rules, sometimes overgeneralising them, and gradually adapting them. Some of the clearest evidence for this process comes from utterances which are unlike anything which the adult would produce, since it is these deviant utterances that reflect most clearly the child's idiosyncratic system. They can offer us, too, hints about the learning strategies and mechanisms which the child is employing.

Attitudes towards second language learners' speech have evolved in very similar ways. Until the late 1960s, most people probably regarded it as a faulty version of the target language. The notion of 'interference' reinforces this view: existing habits prevent correct speech from becoming established; errors are signs of learning failure and, as such, not to be willingly tolerated. However, the new approach to the child's first language encouraged a change of approach in the second language context. The notion developed that second language learners, too, could be viewed as actively constructing rules from the data they encounter and gradually adapting these rules in the direction of the target-language system. If this is so, then the speech of second language learners, like that of the child, can be analysed in its own terms. This means that learners' errors need not be seen as signs of failure. On the contrary, they are the clearest evidence for the learner's developing systems and can offer us insights into how they process the data of the language.

From this perspective, it is no longer surprising if contrastive analysis is limited in its power to predict errors. If learners are actively constructing a system for the second language, we would not expect all their incorrect notions about it to be a simple result of transferring rules from their first language. We would expect many of their incorrect notions to be explicable by direct reference to the target language itself. This is, in fact, precisely what error analysis reveals. In addition to errors due to transferring rules from the mother tongue (sometimes called 'interlingual'

errors), learners also make many errors which show that they are processing the second language in its own terms. Errors of this second type (often
called '*intra*lingual') are often similar to those produced by the child in
the mother tongue and suggest that the second language learner is
employing similar strategies, notably generalisation and simplification.

In the next sections, we will look at some examples of intralingual and
interlingual errors. From these errors, which represent the *product* of
learning, we can also gather hints about the underlying *process* of
learning.

The examples are drawn from studies of both children and adults
learning a second language, sometimes with and sometimes without the
help of formal instruction. Though I use the word 'speech' to describe the
utterances, these are sometimes from written data.

## 3.2   Overgeneralisation

The majority of intralingual errors are instances of the same process of
overgeneralisation that has been observed in first language acquisition.

Generalisation is, of course, a fundamental learning strategy in all
domains, not only in language. In order to make sense of our world, we
allocate items to categories; on the basis of these categories, we construct
'rules' which predict how the different items will behave. Sometimes,
however, our predictions are wrong, probably for one of two main
reasons:

a)   For some reason, the rule does not apply to this particular item, even
     though we have allocated the item to the appropriate category. We
     must therefore learn an *exception* to the general rule.
b)   The item belongs to a different category, which is covered by another
     rule. We must therefore either reallocate the item to a different
     category which we know, or we must construct a *new category and
     rule*.

In either case, our initial error was due to *over*generalisation of the rule
which caused the wrong prediction.

First, an example from the non-linguistic world. We allocate a certain
group of animals to the category 'bird' and learn that they share various
features of behaviour, including the habit of flying. When we encounter a
new kind of bird, our 'rule' enables us to assume that it will have the same
habit. If the bird happens to be a penguin, however, this assumption will
be an error. We will have overgeneralised our rule and must now learn an
exception. On another occasion, we encounter a bat. Because the bat flies,
we allocate it to the category 'bird'. On this basis, we predict other forms
of bird-like behaviour, such as the ability to lay eggs. Again, we have
made an error of overgeneralisation. This time, however, we do not learn

an exception, but allocate the animal to a different category 'mammal', which is governed by different rules.

Here are examples of language-learning equivalents of these errors:

1 A learner of English (as a first or second language) has learnt a rule for forming plurals. This lets him predict that a noun can be made plural by adding *s*. However, when he says *We saw two mouses*, he has overgeneralised the rule, since *mouse* is one of the exceptions to it. In a similar way, until he learns that *come* and *go* lie outside the scope of the general rule for forming the past tense, he is likely to produce overgeneralised forms such as *comed* and *goed*.

2 A learner of French has learnt a rule for forming the perfect tense. This enables him to produce *J'ai fini, J'ai vendu*, and many other forms. Using this rule, he produces *J'ai parti* and *J'ai descendu*. Again, he has overgeneralised the rule and produced errors. This time, however, he should not learn exceptions. He has to learn that the verbs *partir* and *descendre* belong to a special category of verbs which are governed by a different rule for forming the past tense, giving *Je suis parti* and *Je suis descendu*.

These particular errors are, in fact, frequently made by learners of English and French.

As I said above, the errors themselves are the *product* of learning. From them, we can make inferences about the *process*. The errors are errors of 'overgeneralisation', and it is common to use the same label to describe the learning strategy that they allow us to infer. However, it is more precise to say that the strategy is one of generalisation. It is normally only with the benefit of further knowledge that the learner can realise that it was actually an instance of *over*generalisation.

Below are some examples of overgeneralisation errors, produced by learners of English, French and German. The English data are from studies by M. P. Jain (1974) and Barry Taylor (1975). The French and German examples are from my own data.

OVERGENERALISATION ERRORS: ENGLISH

1 We are not knowing the rules. (Overgeneralised use of the rule for forming progressives.)
2 This shows that how sensitive he is. (Overgeneralised use of *that* for introducing a noun clause.)
3 Who can Angela sees? (Overgeneralised third-person ending.)
4 Who did write this book? (Overgeneralisation of the rule for inserting *do* into interrogatives.)
5 You are not expected to make noise here. (*Noise* is classed as 'uncount-able', so *a* is omitted.)

OVERGENERALISATION ERRORS: FRENCH

1 J'entends quelqu'un frappe à la porte. (Third-person verb form used after *quelqu'un*, but the infinitive is needed here.)
2 Il fait du beau jour. (Compare *Il fait du soleil* etc.)
3 Vous avez gagné une voiture nouvelle rouge. (The rule which places most adjectives after their noun is overgeneralised to *nouvelle*.)
4 Peux-je il téléphoner? (Overgeneralised use of *peux* and *il*.)
5 Vous disez votre père n'est pas ici. (*Disez* would be the expected form by analogy: c.f. *lisons/lisez* and others. This sentence also contains an example of transfer – see next section.)

OVERGENERALISATION ERRORS: GERMAN

1 Julia habe gern das Land. (Overgeneralised use of first-person-singular verb ending.)
2 Wir haben Tischtennis gespielen. (Past participle formed on the pattern of many 'irregular' verbs.)
3 Da war eine Party und war ich spät nach Hause. (Inversion of subject and verb is inappropriate after *und*.)
4 Ich habe nach Hause um halb eins gekommen. (Past-tense formation with *haben* overgeneralised to *kommen*, which requires *sein*.)
5 Dann ein Polizeiauto entlang die Strasse komme. (Several errors, including overgeneralised first-person-singular verb and overgeneralised use of a rule placing the main verb at the end of a subordinate, not main, clause.)

## 3.3 Transfer

Transfer and overgeneralisation are not distinct processes. Indeed, they represent aspects of the same underlying learning strategy. Both result from the fact that the learner uses what he already knows about language, in order to make sense of new experience. In the case of overgeneralisation, it is his previous knowledge of the second language that the learner uses. In the case of transfer, the learner uses his previous *mother-tongue* experience as a means of organising the second language data. It is significant that Barry Taylor found transfer errors to be more frequent with beginners than with intermediate students. The beginner has less previous second language knowledge to draw on in making hypotheses about rules, and might therefore be expected to make correspondingly more use of his first language knowledge.

It is, of course, economical and productive for second language learners to transfer their previous knowledge of language (including the first language) to the new task. It means that they do not have to discover everything from zero. As Pit Corder expresses it, the first language provides a 'rather rich and specific set of hypotheses' (1978, p. 79) which learners can use. For many aspects of the second language, these hypotheses will be confirmed, because of the similarities that languages share. The second language learner is likely to feel that everything he learns is different from his mother tongue, whereas in fact there are many ways in which his mother-tongue knowledge can be directly transferred. For example, in the case of the Spanish-speaking learner of English or the English-speaking learner of French, the basic word-order rules and the main grammatical categories are immediately familiar.

Here are examples of transfer errors, taken from my own data:

### TRANSFER ERRORS: ITALIAN- AND GERMAN-SPEAKING LEARNERS OF ENGLISH

1 We think to come by car. (Italian construction after *pensare* transferred to English.)
2 It's a long time she helps me with the home. (Use of Italian construction for expressing duration from the past into the present.)
3 I promised it to you at the telephone. (German: *am Telefon.*)
4 David always fools so much about. (*About* placed at the end of the clause like a German 'separable prefix'.)
5 Jan sleeps long. (Tense and adverb as in German: *Jan schläft lange.*)

### TRANSFER ERRORS: ENGLISH-SPEAKING LEARNERS OF FRENCH

1 Puis-je aider vous? (English position for object pronoun.)
2 Je suis fait mon devoir. (Attempt to form a 'present continuous' tense on the pattern of English.)
3 Je vais et ouvre la porte. (Compare *I go and open . . .*)
4 Elle montre Madame Rouchon les examples. (Two unmarked objects can follow English *show* but not French *montre.*)
5 Je suis pardon. (Compare English *I am sorry.*)

### TRANSFER ERRORS: ENGLISH-SPEAKING LEARNERS OF GERMAN

1 Heute er findet eine Spinne. (English word order.)
2 Ich war gerade gehen in der Café. (Compare English: *I was just going . . .*)
3 Unsere Familie fahren auf dem Lande. (English, but not German, allows a plural verb after *family.*)

4  Warst du da alles Abend? (Compare English: *all evening.*)
5  Er bekam sehr zornig. (Compare English: *He became . . .*)

With some of the examples above, it could also be argued that over-generalisation is at work. *We think to come*, for example, could be a case of overgeneralisation from the pattern in *We expect to come*. A large number of errors are, in fact, ambiguous as to their source. I will discuss this briefly in the next section.

## 3.4   Ambiguous source of many errors

There are many instances when it is not possible to decide whether over-generalisation or transfer is the cause of a specific error. Even some of the examples of overgeneralisation discussed earlier could be reinterpreted as transfer. Thus, *J'ai parti* could be seen not only as overgeneralised use of a French rule for forming the perfect tense with *avoir*, but also as transfer of the English 'have + past participle' rule (c.f. *He has gone*). Likewise, when a German speaker of English heard her child being naughty in another room and asked *Are you stupid there, Jan?* (instead of *Are you being stupid . . .?*), this could be seen either as overgeneralisation of the English rule that usually prevents *to be* from occurring in the present progressive form (as in *Are you tired?*), or as transfer from German, where there is no special progressive form. The same speaker said on another occasion *Did it strike you to be funny?* This is similarly ambiguous. It could either be seen as overgeneralisation of the English pattern which could occur after *seem* (*Did it seem to you to be funny?*), or as transfer of an equivalent German pattern (*Schien es dir, komisch zu sein?*).

In cases such as these, it may be pointless to speculate on which process may be the primary cause. It is equally probable that both processes might occur simultaneously and reinforce each other. For example, the exist-ence of an English past form with *have* may encourage a learner to over-generalise the French form with *avoir*; or the fact that *to be* is not often found in its progressive form may encourage the process of transfer of the German simple form. Indeed, this kind of dual influence seems highly probable, especially in view of the basic similarity between over-generalisation and transfer (c.f. section 3.3).

So many errors seem to be attributable to either (or both) of these two processes that we may feel sceptical of some of the categorisations found in published studies, where the majority of errors are attributed unam-biguously to one source or the other. We may then wonder why, for example, Barry Taylor categorises one instance of incorrect negative placement as overgeneralisation (*Ricardo had not the tickets*), but another as transfer (*Ricardo has not the tickets last night*). Similarly, some of the instances of transfer mentioned in a study by Larry Selinker et al. (1975) could equally well be categorised as overgeneralisation (e.g. *Le chien a mangé les*: transfer from English, or perhaps also overgeneralisation of the usual subject-verb-object order in French?).

Such uncertainty must also make us query, of course, many of the figures which researchers have given concerning the proportion of errors due to transfer and overgeneralisation. It may be that the psychological reality of second language learning makes such figures invalid in any case.

## 3.5 Simplification by omission

We saw that overgeneralisation and transfer can both be seen as expressions of the same underlying strategy of applying previous knowledge to the second language learning task. They can also both be seen as forms of simplification. Through them, the confusing variety of linguistic data is made more manageable, by fitting it into a framework of categories and rules that the learner already possesses.

The order which learners create is not only simpler to manage. It is also more productive, because the categories and rules can be used to create new utterances for expressing new meanings. Jürgen Meisel (1980) has used the term 'elaborative simplification' to describe this process, because it contributes to the learner's development of an underlying system. It is the result of constructive hypotheses about the second language and a sign of progression. We also saw this in connection with the child's apparent regression, which was actually a progression, from *went* and *came* to *goed* and *comed* (chapter 1, section 1.5.2).

There is another form of simplification which seems to be less productive in this sense. This is the kind of simplification which we saw in children's telegraphic speech. The omission of inflections and other morphemes seems to be due more to limitations in capacity than to the construction of rules. Rules are being developed, of course, but these govern relationships between words rather than the process of omission. The latter serves mainly an indirect function, by releasing capacity which the learner can devote to other aspects of the learning process.

This kind of simplification is sometimes called 'redundancy reduction', because it eliminates many items which are redundant to conveying the intended message. For example, the omission of the verb inflection and the article in *daddy want chair* does not prevent the meaning from being understood. Provided that the situation supplies the missing elements of meaning, much greater reduction can take place, as we saw with utterances such as *mommy sock*. Redundancy reduction makes production easier but may, of course, make comprehension difficult or even impossible.

Here are some examples from second language speech. They are taken from studies of a child learner of English (Huang and Hatch, 1978), an adolescent learner of English (Butterworth and Hatch, 1978) and a child learner of German (Pienemann, 1980):

CHILD LEARNER OF ENGLISH (aged five)

1 This kite. (Also possible transfer from Taiwanese, which does not need *to be*.)
2 Wash hand?
3 Ball doggy?

ADOLESCENT LEARNER OF ENGLISH

1 No understand. (Also possible transfer of Spanish rule.)
2 He champion.
3 Is man. (Also possible transfer of Spanish rule.)

CHILD LEARNER OF GERMAN (aged eight)

1 Ich Italiener.
2 Ein Mädchen Bier. (pointing to a girl drinking beer)
3 Bonbon. (pointing to a girl eating a sweet)

It is once again clear that the different processes overlap and may work together. Thus in three of the examples above, the omission of elements could also be attributed to the effects of transfer from the mother tongue, where the elements in question are not obligatory. There are also many cases when it is not possible to distinguish between redundancy reduction due to omission (as discussed here) and the effects of overgeneralisation, which may be the same. For example, the verb form in *He go for café* or *He understand chess* can be seen both as redundancy reduction by omitting the third-person ending, and as overgeneralisation of the form used after *I, we,* and so on.

## 3.6 Learning processes: summary

By looking at the kinds of error that learners make, we have seen evidence for three main processes:

1 transfer of rules from the mother tongue;
2 generalisation (and overgeneralisation) of second language rules;
3 redundancy reduction by omitting elements.

The first of these is an 'interlingual' process. The second and third are 'intralingual'.

We have also seen how the processes are not distinct. Transfer and overgeneralisation are expressions of the same underlying strategy of using previous knowledge to understand new experience. Redundancy reduction can coincide with transfer and overgeneralisation. All three processes can be seen as forms of simplification. Not surprisingly, then, it is often not possible to attribute a particular error unambiguously to one single cause. In fact, it may be part of the normal psychological reality of second language learning that the three processes work together and reinforce each other.

It seems likely that the main creative processes which underlie second language learning are transfer and generalisation. Simplification through omission would appear to have a less directly creative role. However, it may perform an important function in ensuring that the learner can devote more of his available learning capacity to other aspects of his developing language system.

The role of imitation cannot be assessed on the basis of analysing errors. We will return to it in another context, in chapter 4 (section 4.6).

## 3.7 Non-systematic errors

One of the claims made about errors, as we have seen in this chapter, is that they help us to see how learners process the second language and develop underlying systems of rules. The assumption is that the speech which they produce is a direct reflection of the rules which they have internalised, that is, of their underlying 'competence' in the second language.

I must now point out, however, that this assumption is not always justified. Learners may also make errors which do not result from any underlying system, but from more superficial influences. Two such influences may be (a) immediate communication strategies and (b) performance factors.

COMMUNICATION STRATEGIES

There will be occasions when learners are compelled to attempt to express a meaning for which their competence contains no appropriate items or rules at all. In order to get the required meaning across, the learner may then resort to matching language items to the situation in any ad hoc way that will solve his immediate problem. Indeed, even before a person has actually begun to learn a language, it is possible to communicate by using individual items from a dictionary or phrase-book, together with gestures. On occasions such as this, we would scarcely be justified in taking the resulting errors as evidence of an underlying grammatical system. They seem rather to be the outcome of a more general problem-solving strategy, which happens to employ elements from the second language.

This explanation might apply to some of the cases of redundancy reduction discussed in section 3.5. For example, when a learner produces a verbless utterance such as *ein Mädchen Bier*, the omission of the verb may not be evidence for any 'rule' that he has acquired. It may be more appropriate to see him as employing a 'communication strategy' through which, in a specific context, he can convey meanings which would otherwise be beyond his acquired competence. Indeed, many apparent instances of overgeneralisation or transfer may likewise be more the result of an immediate communication strategy than of an underlying system: in order to cope with a communication problem, the learner may consciously have recourse to the mother-tongue system (c.f. transfer) or use second language items which he knows are not completely appropriate (c.f. overgeneralisation).

It is obviously not always possible to determine whether a deviant form is the result of a communication strategy or of an internalised rule. Communication strategies are more likely to occur at the level of consciousness, but consciousness exists in varying degrees. Another possible criterion is whether an error occurs regularly in the learner's speech: the more it is regular, the more it is likely to reflect the underlying system. Again, however, this criterion is not reliable since, as we shall see later (chapter 7, section 7.2), variability is itself a normal feature of learners' speech.

We will look at communication strategies in greater detail in chapter 7 (section 7.3).

PERFORMANCE ERRORS

Even when we speak our mother tongue, we sometimes make errors of performance. We may produce 'slips of the tongue', lose track of a complex structure as we utter it, begin an utterance and abandon it, and so on. The second language learner, too, must inevitably make errors of this nature. Like communication strategies, they cannot be taken as reflections of the learner's developing system, since they are the result of more transitory features of the situation or the learner's performance.

In the terminology of error analysis, such performance errors are sometimes called 'lapses' or 'mistakes', to distinguish them from the more systematic 'errors'. From one single occurrence of a deviant form, it is not possible to distinguish whether it is a systematic error or a non-systematic mistake. As with communication strategies, the most reliable criterion is that of regularity: the best evidence that an error reflects the learner's underlying system is when it appears regularly in his speech. In the case of a mistake, it is also more likely that the learner will be able to recognise the mistake himself and correct it afterwards.

Any attempt to draw a strict borderline between errors and mistakes is unlikely to be successful, since it seems unlikely that they are clearly distinct in their psychological reality. As I said above, variability is itself a normal feature of learners' speech. In other words, even when the system works 'regularly', it produces a lot of surface 'irregularity'. Error analysis is based on the assumption that the product is still sufficiently regular to enable us to make generalisations about the system, and this assumption seems to have been justified in practice. Nonetheless, our neat conclusions are always likely to be confused by sequences such as the following, in which a learner of French produces three different forms for the present tense (two erroneous, one correct) in three lines of her written dialogue:

– Est-ce que votre père ici s'il vous plaît?
– Non, il a travaille.
– Où est-il travaille?
– Il travaille dans un bureau.     (*Il travaille* is correct.)

## 3.8   Errors due to the effects of teaching

If a learner is taking part in formal instruction, some errors will be a direct result of misunderstanding caused by faulty teaching or materials. For example, the distinction between two forms may not be clearly explained, with the result that the learner confuses them. Alternatively, one form or pattern may be overemphasised or overpractised, so that the learner produces it in inappropriate contexts.

As an example of this, Jack Richards (1971) suggests that many teachers or materials place special emphasis on the present continuous form in English. Their purpose is to counteract the fact that if the learners possess no equivalent form in their mother tongue (as is frequently the case), they may be inclined to use it less frequently than they should. However, this extra emphasis may have the undesired effect of making learners *over*-use the continuous form, at the expense of the simple present. In a similar way, frequent drilling of French patterns with *en* (e.g. *Il y en a deux*) sometimes causes learners to include it even when the noun is mentioned (e.g. *Il y en a deux hommes*).

These errors are basically a special instance of overgeneralisation errors, which were discussed in section 3.2. They are particularly interesting in that a specific cause for the overgeneralisation can be identified in the language 'input' which the learner has received. If we had a record of all the language to which a learner has been exposed, we would perhaps be able to attribute some other instances of overgeneralisation to similar external sources, such as the frequency with which a particular form occurs in the input or the misleading juxtaposition of two forms.

## 3.9 Some terminology

In order to describe the language of second language learners, a number of terms have become current. They refer to the same phenomenon, but emphasise different aspects.

If we wish to focus on the fact that learners are developing their underlying knowledge of the second language, we can use the term *transitional competence* (Corder, 1967). This describes the system of rules that a learner has developed at a particular stage (his 'competence') and emphasises its temporary nature as the learner progresses.

We can also view the learner as speaking an *idiosyncratic dialect* (Corder, 1971). This term emphasises that at any given time, the learner operates a self-contained language variety ('dialect'). However, compared with the dialect of normal speech communities, many more aspects of this language will be unique ('idiosyncratic') to the individual learner–speaker.

Another term which describes the learner's language is *approximative system* (Nemser, 1971). This draws attention to structural aspects of the learner's language, which 'approximates' more or less closely to the full second language system.

The term which has been used most frequently of all is *interlanguage*, often abbreviated to IL (Selinker, 1972). It draws attention to the fact that the learner's language system is neither that of the mother tongue, nor that of the second language, but contains elements from both. If we imagine a continuum between the first language system (which constitutes the learner's initial knowledge) and the second language system (which is his target), we can say that at any given time, the learner speaks an 'interlanguage' (IL) at some point along this continuum.

In addition to the terms above, which highlight various aspects of the learner's language, a reader is also likely to encounter more neutral terms, such as *learner English* (or *learner German*, and so on) or *language-learner language*.

## 3.10 Fossilisation

Normally, we expect a learner to progress further along the learning continuum, so that his 'interlanguage' moves closer and closer to the target language system and contains fewer and fewer errors. However, some errors will probably never disappear entirely. Such errors are often described as *fossilised*, meaning that they have become permanent features of the learner's speech. Obvious examples are the pronunciation errors which form part of the 'foreign accent' retained by most adolescent and adult learners. Many of the unique features of immigrant dialects derive originally from errors which fossilised, first at the individual level and then in the speech community.

If we wish, then, we can make a distinction between 'transitional' errors (which eventually disappear, as the learner progresses) and 'fossilised' errors (which do not disappear entirely). It has been suggested that even if the influence of the mother tongue is less strong than was once assumed in determining what errors learners make, it may still be the major influence in determining which errors fossilise. A further suggestion is that fossilisation is most likely to occur when a learner realises (subconsciously) that the error does not hinder him in satisfying his communicative needs (at the functional or social level). A learner who feels only rudimentary communicative needs is therefore likely to stop progressing at an earlier stage than a learner with a fuller range of needs. We will return to this suggestion later, in chapters 5 (section 5.3) and 6 (section 6.2.1).

Apart from suggestions such as these, we clearly have little knowledge of what causes some errors to fossilise, rather than others.

## 3.11 The learner's internal syllabus

As we have seen, one of the most important conclusions drawn from error analysis is that the learner approaches the learning task with active strategies, notably generalisation and transfer, which help him to construct the rules which underlie the second language. This is the 'creative construction hypothesis'.

Even if we accept that the creative construction hypothesis is valid, it would still be possible for each learner to apply the strategies in different ways and proceed through different stages in learning the language. From what we know about first language acquisition and other areas of human learning, however, we must also admit a strong possibility that the application of similar strategies will predispose learners to follow similar learning sequences. According to this hypothesis, it is often said that second language learners may be endowed with an 'internal syllabus' (or 'built-in syllabus') for learning the language. Provided that their natural processes have scope to operate, the internal syllabus will determine, to a large extent, the learning path that they will follow.

The classroom learner is, of course, also provided with an *external* syllabus, in which items have been placed into a teaching sequence. This may conflict with the learner's internal syllabus, but will not necessarily override it. That is, the learner may still be employing his natural strategies in order to process the data and actually to internalise it: the *learning* sequence may not be the same as the teaching sequence. This may not be evident from observing the controlled performance which learners produce in many classroom exercises. These have often been artificially constructed in order to elicit specific items which have been taught. However, it may become evident when the learner is placed into an uncontrolled situation, where he has to use the language more freely and spontaneously, for the communication of meanings.

The idea of the internal syllabus is supported by the fact that learners make similar kinds of errors, irrespective of what course of instruction they have followed or whether they have received formal instruction at all. It is also supported by a number of empirical studies, which have examined the sequences which learners have followed in mastering various aspects of the second language system. It is to these studies that we will turn in the next chapter.

## 3.12  Summary

In this chapter, we have seen how the study of learners' errors shows that second language learning is more than a simple matter of habit-formation. We have seen evidence that second language learners use creative strategies which are not dissimilar from those used by first language learners. The most important of these strategies seem to be generalisation, transfer and other forms of simplification. However, we do not understand the learning process sufficiently well to be able to state which strategy is most likely to be applied at a particular stage or in a particular domain of language. In any case, in their deeper psychological reality, the strategies are probably not distinct from each other.

Some errors seem to be produced by performance factors or communication strategies, rather than by the rules of the learner's underlying system. Some errors seem to be induced by specific teaching techniques. In these areas too, however, no clear distinctions can be drawn.

We have seen a number of different terms that are used to describe the language of second language learners. The different stages which learners pass through may be determined, to some extent, by an 'internal syllabus'. We will look more closely at this idea in the next chapter.

# 4 The internal syllabus of the language learner

## 4.1 Introduction

As we saw in the previous chapter, the study of errors suggests some ways in which learners actively construct their knowledge of the second language. We also saw that the term 'internal syllabus' has been used to indicate that there may be a psychologically natural path for learners to take as they master the language. In this chapter, we will examine some more of the evidence for this idea. We will look at studies of the sequences followed by learners in acquiring various aspects of the second language.

The learners in these studies include both children and adults. In some cases, but not all, they have received formal instruction in the second language. There is still a lot of debate surrounding the question of how much these factors – age and instruction – affect sequences of learning. As we shall see, there is evidence that they have less effect than we sometimes assume.

One common feature of the learners in the studies is that they have all lived in the second language environment and therefore been exposed to the language in 'real-life' situations. This means that they have needed to use the second language for communication and have therefore experienced, to some degree at least, the natural stimulus to learn language that also underlies first language acquisition. Again, this may be an important factor in activating natural processes and determining learning sequences. A reader who teaches a language outside the country where it is spoken may therefore wonder whether the studies are relevant to his or her learners. I would suggest that there are two major reasons why they are:

1   If there are natural processes for second language learning, these will form part of the learner's psychological make-up in every learning situation, including the classroom. The teacher can therefore benefit by knowing about these processes and trying to work with rather than against them. For example, knowledge of natural sequences and strategies may help us to devise more appropriate teaching sequences, more successful methods of presentation, or a more beneficial approach to correcting errors.

2   If there are, indeed, specific features of the learning situation which

activate these natural processes, we can explore whether the same features can (or should) be reproduced in the classroom setting. For example, studies of natural second language learning have helped to support the need to create realistic contexts for communicative language use in the classroom. They have also helped to focus attention on some of the psychological factors which support or inhibit second language learning.

In the present chapter, we will look first at some studies which have examined sequences for learning grammatical morphemes. We will then look at studies which have focussed on the learning of other grammatical structures.

## 4.2   Learning grammatical morphemes

In chapter 1, we looked at studies of how children acquire grammatical morphemes in English as a first language. Of particular importance are the 'longitudinal' study of Roger Brown (1973) and the 'cross-sectional' study of Jill and Peter de Villiers (1973), which suggest that children acquire fourteen of these morphemes in a natural sequence. These studies have stimulated similar work in the second language context.

The most widely discussed studies of morpheme acquisition sequences in a second language were carried out by Heidi Dulay and Marina Burt, whom I also mentioned at the end of chapter 2. Like most other second language researchers, Dulay and Burt used the cross-sectional design. That is, they took samples from a large number of learners at one point in time, scored each morpheme for accuracy in the learners' speech, and drew up an accuracy order for the morphemes. Rightly or wrongly (c.f. chapter 1, section 1.5.2, also 4.2.1 below), they assumed that this accuracy order reflected the acquisition order for the morphemes.

Dulay and Burt first (1973) studied eight morphemes in the speech of three different groups of Spanish-speaking children (151 in all, aged between five and eight) who were learning English in the natural environment. They calculated the average accuracy order for each group and found that the order for each of the three groups was very similar. From this, they concluded that Spanish children acquire these morphemes in a natural order. This order is not the same as that of children learning English as their mother tongue, but Dulay and Burt attribute this fact to differences in cognitive maturity.

Soon afterwards, Dulay and Burt carried out a similar study (1974b) of the English speech of two groups with different mother tongues: sixty Spanish-speaking children and fifty-five Chinese-speaking children. This time, they examined eleven morphemes. Again, they found that the accuracy order was similar for the two groups. They concluded from this that the natural order for acquiring morphemes is independent of the learners' mother tongue. In other words, first language transfer (or 'interference') is not a major factor; the sequence is not only natural, but also universal.

Nathalie Bailey et al. (1974) carried out a similar study with seventy-three adults. They divided the learners into two groups: those whose native language was Spanish and those with other mother tongues. Again, the researchers calculated an average accuracy order for the speech of each group and, again, they found that the groups showed a similar order. Indeed, not only were the two groups similar to each other (suggesting that mother tongue had no significant effect): they were also similar to the Spanish-speaking children studied by Dulay and Burt (suggesting that age had no significant effect, either).

The results of these studies suggest, then, that second language learners acquire the grammatical morphemes in a natural sequence which is not significantly affected either by age or by mother tongue.

The studies mentioned so far in this section used speech which learners produced in so-called 'structured conversation'. The researchers used a set of pictures and questions (published as the 'Bilingual Syntax Measure' or 'BSM') in order to elicit speech. Another group of researchers, Stephen Krashen et al. (1978), studied the morphemes produced by learners in *written* English, using free essays written by adults of various mother tongues. Yet again, a similar order was found.

Diane Larsen-Freeman (1975) also found a similar order, using the Bilingual Syntax Measure with twenty-four adults with four different mother tongues (Arabic, Japanese, Persian and Spanish). However, when the same learners performed a written task which involved language-manipulation exercises, she found that the order was significantly different. One explanation proposed for this is that any natural acquisition sequence might fail to show itself in tasks where the focus is on manipulating forms rather than expressing meanings. The learner's underlying competence is only tapped when he is involved in using the language for spontaneous communication; a different, more conscious knowledge is used when he is manipulating forms. We will return to this idea in chapter 7, in connection with Krashen's 'monitor model'. In the meantime, we might note that many of the tasks performed in language-teaching classrooms consist of language manipulation rather than communication, and may not offer a true reflection of the learner's underlying knowledge of the language.

Even when we consider only spontaneous communication, of course, the orders revealed by the various studies have not been identical: they have only been similar. The degree of regularity is best captured by showing the observed sequences not as a list of individual morphemes, but as a hierarchy of *groups* of morphemes. We can then say that the morphemes in Group 1 are regularly acquired before those in Group 2, those in Group 2 before those in Group 3, and so on. *Within* each group, however, there is some variation. Using this approach, the average acquisition order for nine morphemes (as calculated by Krashen, 1982) is shown below. It can be compared with the average order for first language learners, given in chapter 1 (section 1.5.2).

*Group 1:*   present progressive -*ing* (as in *boy running*)
            plural -*s* (as in *two books*)
            copula 'to be' (as in *he is big*)
*Group 2:*   auxiliary 'to be' (as in *he is running*)
            articles *the* and *a*
*Group 3:*   irregular past forms (as in *she went*)
*Group 4:*   regular past -*ed* (as in *she climbed*)
            third-person-singular -*s* (as in *she runs*)
            possessive -*s* (as in *man's hat*).

Various explanations for this order have been suggested. According to Larsen-Freeman (1976), it reflects the frequency with which the morphemes occur in the speech of native speakers. Other influences may be how clearly the morphemes are perceived in the flow of sound ('perceptual saliency') and how important they are to the communication of meaning.

From the studies which have been discussed in this section, then, a neat picture emerges. It suggests that, with some differences of detail, a number of English morphemes are acquired in a predictable, 'natural' sequence. The sequence seems to be similar whether the learners are children or adults, whatever their mother tongue, and even if they have received some formal instruction (as in the case of the adults in the studies described above). However, a condition for perceiving this order is that we tap the learners' underlying competence, through tasks which require them to focus on the communication of meanings rather than just to manipulate forms.

Before proceeding, however, it is necessary to cast some doubts over this neat picture, since the issues are not so resolved as they might appear.

### 4.2.1   *Learning morphemes: some unresolved problems*

Some of the doubts expressed about the studies discussed in the previous section are:

1   I mentioned earlier that cross-sectional studies are based on the assumption that the *accuracy* order (discovered by analysing the speech of a large number of learners at one point in time) is a reliable

reflection of what the *acquisition* order would be, if we studied individual learners over a real period of time (i.e. in a 'longitudinal' study).

This assumption is not necessarily valid (c.f. chapter 1, section 1.5.2), and many second language researchers do not accept it. Indeed, Ellen Rosansky (1976) tested the assumption, by comparing the actual acquisition order for one learner (studied over time) with the same learner's accuracy order at single points in time. She did not find a significant correlation. However, Rosansky's results have themselves been subjected to criticism, and the issue remains unresolved.

2   The arguments for a natural, universal sequence are not supported by the longitudinal study carried out by Kenji Hakuta (1974a). Hakuta followed the development of a five-year-old Japanese girl learning English, and found a sequence which was different from that of Dulay and Burt. Most noticeably, plurals and articles were acquired considerably later. Hakuta points out that the notion of plurality and the definite/indefinite distinction (expressed by the articles) do not exist in Japanese grammar. If this is the reason for their late acquisition, it means that the mother tongue has a greater influence than suggested by the studies in the previous section. This is also suggested by Ann Fathman's study (1979), in which Korean and Spanish learners were significantly different in acquiring the articles.

Although studies such as these raise doubts about the existence of a *universal* order for learning the morphemes, they do not necessarily affect the argument that a learner may have a psychologically *natural* order, which is determined partly by his previous mother-tongue knowledge. In fact, they would seem to support the general conclusions drawn from error analysis and discussed in chapter 3: that learning is guided partly by the learner's mother-tongue knowledge (e.g. transfer) and partly by factors independent of the mother tongue.

3   Another worry is connected with the method which was used to elicit speech in most of the studies: the Bilingual Syntax Measure (BSM). The questions and prompts, which accompany the pictures, may exert their own influence on the speech that learners produce. For example, if the interviewer says 'Show me the . . .', the learner's answer is likely to copy the definite article from this model, whether or not the article would have occurred in free speech. The resulting data may therefore give the impression that the article is more fully mastered than is really the case.

One study which supports this argument was conducted by John Porter (1977). Porter used the BSM to elicit speech from *first* language learners. If the BSM is a neutral measure of competence, one would expect it to reveal an order similar to that found in other first language studies. In fact, Porter found that the children's accuracy order was closer to that of *second* language learners tested with the BSM, suggesting that the order in all these studies might have been strongly influenced by the BSM.

On the other hand, the order revealed by the BSM has been supported by studies using other methods, as we have already seen. These other methods include essay writing (Krashen et al.), spontaneous speech (Krashen et al. – but Rosansky found a different order) and an elicitation procedure called the SLOPE test (Fathman). We can again only conclude that the issue is unresolved and that there is room for a lot more research.

4  Other researchers have cast doubt on the morpheme studies for more technical reasons. One of these concerns the way in which morphemes are categorised for the purpose of analysis. For example, when researchers place *a* and *the* into the single category 'article', they obscure the fact that different learners may acquire these in a different order. A similar criticism concerns the way in which scores are calculated for large groups of learners rather than individuals: again, individual variation would not be revealed. Rosansky has shown, in fact, that the group averages for morpheme accuracy conceal a large range of variation, in first language as well as second language studies.

5  Finally, when using the morpheme studies to draw conclusions about the process of second language learning – for example, as evidence for creative construction or natural learning sequences – we should remember that the studies have so far been almost entirely limited to English. We need confirmatory evidence from other languages before we can be confident in making generalisations about second language learning as a human phenomenon.

Despite the many unresolved issues, however, we can say that there is evidence that second language learners have a strong tendency to acquire a set of English morphemes in a predictable order. There is also evidence for variation between learners, caused either by the mother tongue or by individual factors.

## 4.3    Learning to form negatives

There have been several longitudinal studies of the development of English negatives in learners' speech. Roar Ravem (1968, 1978) and Henning Wode (1976) studied, respectively, two Norwegian-speaking children and four German-speaking children. Marilyn Adams (1978) looked at ten Spanish-speaking children. Herlinda Cancino et al. (1978) looked at six native speakers of Spanish: two children, two adolescents and two adults. In all of the studies, the learners were living in an English-speaking environment and learning without formal instruction. The different studies show a considerable degree of similarity in the sequences followed, together with some variation due partly to individual factors and partly to the influence of the mother tongue.

In the account that follows, I take the main framework from Cancino et al., who divide the development into four main stages. It should be stressed, however, that there is never an abrupt transition between stages. There is considerable overlap, with several forms existing together at any one time. Cancino et al. determined the stages according to which form was most frequent at the various times of data-collection.

STAGE 1

In the first stage, the most common pattern for producing negative utterances is simply to place the negative element (*no* or *not*) before the verb. The Spanish-speaking learners use mostly *no*:

They no have water.
I no sing it.

The Norwegian speakers use mostly *not*:

I not like that.
I not looking for edge.

This preference for *no* or *not* presumably reflects the difference between Spanish and Norwegian. Another instance of mother-tongue transfer was found by Wode: it appears that only the German-speaking children sometimes produce utterances where the negative element follows the main verb (as it does in German):

John go not to school.

Cancino et al. also point out that Spanish influence may explain why the '*no* + verb' pattern is very persistent in their learners' speech: it does not disappear until the final stage. Indeed, it never disappeared entirely from the speech of one of the learners. This reminds us of the suggestion in chapter 3 (section 3.10), that transfer may be the most important factor in determining which errors 'fossilise'.

The studies also give evidence for individual variation at this stage. For example, Adams noted that nine learners used *not* instead of *no* when the copula was required, but one learner used *no* all the time (e.g. *He no was here*). Wode notes that two of his four learners used *nothing* as a negative element before a noun (e.g. *I got nothing shoe*).

STAGE 2

In the second stage, *no* or *not* come to be dominated by *don't*. The form is not yet varied to mark different persons or tenses (*doesn't*, *didn't* do not occur), and it is used before modals such as *can*: this suggests that the learners are using it as a simple alternative to *no* or *not*, rather than as a productive structure consisting of *do* + *not*. For example:

He don't like it.

I don't can explain.

STAGE 3

The next stage which emerges from the studies is that the learners begin to place the negative element after auxiliary verbs such as *is* and *can*:

You can't tell her.

Somebody is not coming in.

When these forms appear, *don't* still seems to be an unanalysed form and is not yet inflected.

STAGE 4

In the fourth stage, *do* performs its full function as a marker of tense and person:

It doesn't spin.

We didn't have a study period.

Did you not say it to daddy?

For a time, however, the tense may be marked on both the auxiliary and the main verb:

He didn't found it.

She doesn't wants it.

This division into stages gives an oversimplified picture of the development and exaggerates its neatness and regularity. As I said earlier, the stages are not separated in reality, and a learner may use a number of forms at one point in time. Also, it is clearly impossible to specify precisely when *don't* becomes a productive, analysed structure (*do* + *not*), rather than a single element equivalent to *no* or *not*. Despite a lot of fuzziness and uncertainty, however, the evidence suggests that learners tend to follow a similar sequence as they acquire the negative. There also seems to be some influence from the learners' mother tongue and, within a group of learners with the same mother tongue, a certain amount of individual variation.

If we glance back at chapter 1 (section 1.5.3), we can also see that the typical second language sequence shares a number of common features with the sequence observed in first language learners. In particular, these include the stage when the negative element is simply inserted before the verb, and the use of *don't* as an uninflected particle. A first language stage which has not been observed clearly in second language learning is the initial one, when the negative particle is placed outside the sentence.

However, isolated examples were noted by Adams and Wode (*no dis one no, no play baseball*). We might note here that some researchers do not believe that this stage always occurs in first language acquisition, either: they argue that in utterances like *no singing song*, the child is simply omitting the subject.

## 4.4 Learning to form questions

In addition to studying the development of negatives in their learners' speech, Adams, Cancino et al. and Ravem examined the development of questions. Again, they observed similar sequences amongst their various learners, together with some variation due to the mother tongue and to individual factors.

For the present account, I will take the main framework from Adams, who distinguishes three main stages both for wh-questions and for yes/no questions. As with negatives, of course, there are no sudden transitions in the learners' actual development, so that the stages overlap considerably.

STAGE I

The first stage is similar to that for negatives, in that learners form their questions with the minimum possible disturbance of the basic sentence structure.

With yes/no questions, they use the declarative word order and signal the question by intonation, without inversion:

Wanna see something?
I did good?

This device is, of course, also used by native speakers.

With wh-questions, too, the declarative word order is retained. The question word is simply placed at the front of the sentence, again without inversion:

What she is doing?
Why we not live in Scotland?

This stage is identical to the initial stage observed in first language acquisition.

STAGE 2

In the second stage, inversion sometimes takes place but sometimes does not. It first occurs regularly with *to be* and *can*.

According to Adams, the first use of inversion with *do* is in routine expressions, such as *Do you know?*, which have probably been learnt as fixed phrases – an instance where imitation rather than rule-formation is at work. Ravem concludes that *do* first emerges as a kind of prefix attached to *you*, which produces not only correct-sounding utterances such as *What d'you like?*, but also overt errors such as *What d'you reading?* In one of her learners, Adams found a similar use of *do* as a general question marker, resulting in a similar mixture of erroneous and correct-sounding utterances:

> Do you wanna play bingo?
> Do you can bring it?
> Do you brought your lunch?

In all of these cases, then, *do* appears in the learners' speech before they have actually mastered the appropriate rule for forming questions with it. This was also the sequence with negative *don't*.

We have just seen one example of individual variation. Ravem provides us with another, in which there also seems to be transfer from the mother tongue. He found that one of his learners produced some yes/no questions by inverting the subject and the main verb, on the Norwegian pattern (e.g. *Drive you car to-yesterday?*). He did not find this with wh-questions, however.

STAGE 3

In the third stage, the use of inversion spreads. It becomes regular with *to be* and all modal verbs. In addition, the learners develop a productive ability to form questions by using an appropriate form of *do*, inverted with the subject:

> Why doesn't Toto cry?
> What did you do before you get to bed?

As with negatives, there are also instances where the tense is marked twice (e.g. *Where did he found it?*).

In learning to form questions, then, there seems to be a sequence of development which is generally typical of most learners, both children and adults, who are learning through natural processes. This sequence shows a number of similar features to that observed for negatives. It is also similar in many respects to that followed by first language learners (c.f. chapter 1, section 1.5.3). At the same time, there are some signs of variation, due to the mother tongue and to individual factors.

## 4.5   Learning the basic sentence pattern

There has been less detailed study of how learners acquire the ability to form basic affirmative sentences. The clearest evidence for an ordered, 'natural' development comes from Germany, where there have been a number of studies of immigrant adults and children learning German.

Manfred Pienemann (1980) carried out a longitudinal study of three Italian-speaking children, who were aged eight at the beginning of the study. In the early stages of development, he found that the learners' utterances gradually expanded in length. After some time, a sentence might have several constituent phrases, without departing from a basic sequence of subject + verb + object + adverbial(s) (in which not every slot need be filled, of course). For example:

> Bonbon. (c.f. chapter 3, section 3.5)
> Meine Mutter putze.
> Die Kinder spielen mim Ball.
> Ich geh in Spielplatz mit meine Vater und meine Mami.

Apart from the many errors with verb-endings and case-inflections, deviant utterances frequently occur through the omission of obligatory elements:

> Ein Junge Ball weg. (verb and article omitted)

– and through failure to carry out obligatory operations on word order, such as the movement of the past participle to the final position:

> Mein Vater hat gekaufen ein Buch.

One learner (Luigina) never departs from this basic pattern. As the other two (Concetta and Eva) progress, they begin to carry out some of the permutations allowed or required by German grammar. First, they begin to place adverbials at the front of the sentence, but do not invert the subject and verb as the grammar requires:

> Da Kinder spielen.
> Dann ich schreiben?

The obligatory inversion begins with stereotyped phrases such as *Hier ist* . . ., before spreading to other sentence types, where it occurs with increasing regularity:

> Heute kommt noch einmal meine Kusine.
> Und da kommt Polizei.

As this development takes place, the learners are also acquiring the rule which places participles and infinitives at the end of the sentence:

> Ich habe mal gemacht.
> Alle Kinder muss die Pause machen.

As an example of individual variation, Pienemann notes that Concetta never inserts more than one phrase between the two parts of the verb phrase (as in the example above), whereas Eva gradually increases the length of the sequence that can separate the two parts. As a general source of variation, he notes that Concetta is anxious to conform and avoid errors, whereas Eva is more prepared to risk errors in order to communicate more effectively.

## 4.6   Memorising unanalysed formulas and patterns

The previous sections have shown how learners construct systems of rules from which they can create utterances. However, this is not the only way in which learning can take place. In addition, language can become part of a person's repertoire through straightforward imitation and memorisation. The clearest evidence for this is provided by what are sometimes called 'routine formulas' and 'prefabricated patterns'.

A routine formula is an utterance which the learner produces as a single, unanalysed unit, rather than creating it from underlying rules. For example, Joseph Huang and Evelyn Hatch (1978) report that in the first few weeks of learning, a Chinese child (Paul) produced not only simple two-word utterances (such as *this kite* and *wash hand*), but also utterances which seemed to belong to a completely different level of structural ability, for example:

Don't do that.
It's time to eat and drink.
Get out of here.

Significantly, whereas Paul could create a large number of novel utterances based on the simpler two-word patterns, the more complex patterns were not used in other utterances. The child did not say, for example, *Don't eat* or *It's time to wash*. It seems that, through hearing specific utterances on frequent occasions, he had memorised them as complete units and could now produce them himself in situations which called for them. He grasped the meaning globally and knew what communicative function they could perform in appropriate situations. However, he was not aware of their internal structure or of the meaning of their individual components.

Similar to a routine formula is a prefabricated pattern. This has at least one slot which can be filled by alternative items, thus allowing a certain degree of creativity. Again, however, the main body of the utterance exists as a memorised unit. For example, Kenji Hakuta (1974b, 1976) studied a Japanese child (Uguisu) who, after three months of learning, was able to use the pattern *I know how to . . .* with various items in the final slot:

I know how to do it.
I know how to read it this.

The pattern underlying *I know how to . . .* itself was never used creatively. The child did not say, for example, *Tell me how to do it* or *I know when to do it*.

Hakuta noted that, at a later stage, Uguisu produced deviant utterances such as *I know how do you write this*. Superficially, this seemed to mark a step backwards. From the learner's viewpoint, however, it probably indicated that the *creative system* underlying her speech had progressed, almost to the point where *I know how to . . .* could be produced by rules rather than as a memorised unit. In other words, the creative construction process (as discussed in previous sections of this chapter) was almost sufficiently advanced to produce utterances of a type which had so far only been produced in the form of prefabricated patterns.

In addition to the creative system 'catching up' with the patterns produced through imitation, another process may take place. Gradually, routine formulas and prefabricated patterns may become broken up into their separate parts, which can then be used with increasing flexibility and creativity. Lily Wong-Fillmore (1976) found evidence for this process in the speech of Nora, a Spanish child, who showed the following sequence:

1 At an early stage, she used *How do you do dese?* as an invariable routine formula.
2 Later, she began to add other elements to this pattern, e.g. *How do you do dese in English?*
3 This became broken down so that *How do you . . .?* functioned as a prefabricated pattern to which various main verbs could be added, e.g. *How do you like to be a cookie cutter?*
4 Later, *How do you . . .?* was further analysed so that it signalled tense, in alternation with *How did you . . .?*

By the end of this sequence, then, an utterance with *How do you . . .?* could be produced by creative rules rather than imitation.

Additional evidence for the importance of imitation in second language learning comes from a study by Judy Wagner-Gough (1978). This study shows how a Persian child (Homer) uses imitative strategies when interacting with an English native speaker (Judy). For example, an utterance might be imitated but given different intonation, in order to answer a question:

J: Is Misty a cat?
H: Is Misty a cat.   (= 'Yes'.)

An imitated pattern might be broken up by inserting another element:

J: Is it good?
H: Is it yes good.

The imitated pattern may itself be incorporated into a larger pattern:

J:  Where are you going?
H: Where are you going is house.   (= 'I'm going home'.)

In all of the studies mentioned in this section, the learners gave a considerable amount of evidence that they were using imitation and memorisation as strategies for language learning. One reason for this may be that, quite apart from their role in the learning process, imitation and memorisation have a great practical advantage: they can equip learners with items which are valuable for carrying on communication, long before these items could be generated by their underlying linguistic competence.

## 4.7  Summary and conclusion

In this chapter, we have looked at some studies of the sequences which learners have been observed to follow in mastering various aspects of a second language. We have also looked at ways in which they use imitation and memorisation, in addition to creative processes of rule-formation.

We must be wary of generalising too widely from the available evidence, since this is still very limited in scope. Many aspects of language development have not been studied at all; most of the studies are concerned only with the learning of English; and the results need to be confirmed with larger groups of learners, including groups which are more clearly differentiated according to factors that might affect the course of learning (e.g. age, mother tongue and amount of instruction). However, the various studies seem to allow a number of general conclusions, for example:

1 Like first language learners, second language learners tend to follow natural sequences in internalising the system. In main outline, these sequences are similar for different learners, but there is some individual variation in the details of the development.
2 In many respects, these sequences seem to be independent of the learners' mother tongue. They suggest that learners use 'intralingual' strategies which are also found in first language learning, such as generalising rules and reducing redundancy.
3 However, there is also evidence that the learner's mother-tongue knowledge influences the sequences. For example, German learners were found to place *not* after the main verb. From the learners' viewpoint, this strategy ('transfer') is another way of generalising rules acquired by previous learning.
4 As well as forming rules on the basis of the data they are exposed to, learners also imitate and memorise specific utterances, without analysing their internal structure. We should therefore not discard habit-formation principles (c.f. chapter 2) but integrate them into a broader framework.

In general, then, the studies confirm the conclusions drawn from error analysis in chapter 3: (a) that learners construct their knowledge of the second language through active learning processes and (b) that they are inclined to do this according to a natural 'inbuilt syllabus'. The studies also remind us not to ignore the role of processes associated with behaviourism, such as imitation and memorisation.

Our knowledge of these learning processes remains at a very general level, however. For example, we do not know why it is that a particular learner overgeneralises one rule rather than another, or transfers his mother-tongue knowledge in one instance but not in another. Nor, as we shall see in the next chapter, can we make very specific statements about the factors – inside or outside the learner – that might influence the course that learning takes.

# 5 Accounting for differences between learners

## 5.1 Introduction

At several points in the previous chapter, I referred to differences between individual learners. In general, however, the emphasis was on features of development which learners share. Indeed, one of the main conclusions from the discussion was that learners seem inclined to process the language in similar ways.

However, it is common knowledge that learners show greater differences than this conclusion would seem to imply. This is true whether learning is taking place in the classroom or in informal contexts outside the classroom. The precise nature of these differences has not been fully explored. In particular, it is not clear to what extent:

a) there is a single direction of development which all learners follow. Individual differences simply reflect how quickly – or how far – specific learners progress along this common path.

b) individual differences cause learners to progress along different paths of development as they acquire the language.

The evidence of the previous chapter speaks in favour of the first possibility: there seem to be typical sequences of development, from which individual variations are mainly of a minor nature. However, we should remember that this evidence is drawn from a limited number of studies and involves comparatively few areas of development. Also, even though learners show similar sequences in acquiring specific structures, we might still find differences if we took a more global view of their development. For example, one learner might complete his acquisition of structures X and Y simultaneously, whereas another might acquire X much earlier than Y.

Most studies concerned with explaining individual differences do not touch on the precise nature of these differences. They work with a simple notion of varying 'proficiency' in the second language and try to find links between this and non-linguistic factors, such as motivation, intelligence or personality. For example, a researcher might focus on a group of learners and (a) test how highly each learner scores on some non-linguistic measure such as motivation or intelligence, (b) test each learner's proficiency in the second language, and (c) investigate (usually statistically) whether a learner with a high score on the first test is also more likely to have a higher score on the second. If so, we can claim that a high level of motivation or intelligence 'predicts' or 'correlates with' success in language learning. This does not mean that a more intelligent or better motivated person will *necessarily* be more successful but that, on average, he is *more likely* to be so.

## 5.2 Some difficulties in investigating causes for differences

There are many problems that make it difficult to reach firm conclusions about what factors lead to greater proficiency in second language learning. For example:

1 How should we define and measure 'proficiency' in a second language?
 Many different criteria have been used, including classroom grades, performance in multiple-choice tests, imitation of sentences, cloze tests, knowledge of grammar, listening or reading ability, and oral production skills. Note that some of these criteria are of doubtful validity, if we regard language learning as concerning primarily the development of communication skills.
2 How should we measure the non-linguistic factors which we consider likely to affect language learning?
 Studies investigating the influence of the learner's personality have faced this problem in an acute form: there are no convincing methods available for measuring traits such as 'empathy' or 'extroversion'. As a further example, it would be useful to explore exactly how learning is affected by the kind of language to which the learner is exposed, but there are obvious practical difficulties involved in keeping a record of all the language that a learner hears.
3 Even if we are satisfied with our various tests and find a correlation between proficiency and a non-linguistic factor, can we be sure that a direct cause-and-effect relationship is involved?
 The relationship may be indirect. For example, if proficiency correlates with being an extrovert, this may not be due to the extrovert's superiority in actual learning ability. It may simply reflect the fact that he engages in more social interaction and thus has more opportunities to learn. The true causal sequence would thus be: extroversion → social interaction → progress in learning.
 There may be no true causal relationship at all between the two factors measured. For example, let us say that a correlation is found between proficiency and being active in class (e.g. asking and answering a lot of questions). Rather than the activity causing the proficiency, both of these could be caused by some third factor, such as motivation.

4  If we are satisfied that a direct cause-and-effect link exists, can we be
   sure which factor is the cause and which the effect?
      This is a problem in the example just mentioned: motivation might
   lead to greater proficiency, but so might greater proficiency help to
   increase a learner's motivation. As a further example, we may find that
   a learner who is anxious in the classroom makes slower progress. Does
   the anxiety cause the slower progress or vice versa?
      In many cases, including those just mentioned, we are probably
   wrong to look for a one-way relationship at all, since each factor is
   likely to reinforce the other.

With these notes of caution in mind, we will look in the following
sections at some of the non-linguistic factors which many people believe
(from observation and/or statistical evidence) to influence success in
second language learning. I will group them under three main categories
according to whether they relate primarily to: motivation for learning,
opportunities for learning, or ability for learning. This grouping is largely
for convenience and, above all, in the hope of presenting a reasonably
clear picture of a very complex domain. In reality, the categories cannot
be separated so clearly. For example, if a learner has adequate opportunities and ability, these are also likely to help his motivation.


## 5.3   Motivation for learning

In second language learning as in every other field of human learning,
motivation is the crucial force which determines whether a learner
embarks on a task at all, how much energy he devotes to it, and how long
he perseveres. It is a complex phenomenon and includes many
components: the individual's drive, need for achievement and success,
curiosity, desire for stimulation and new experience, and so on. These
factors play a role in every kind of learning situation and I will not deal
with them here. Rather, I will focus on two aspects which are especially
important for second language learning, namely communicative need and
attitudes towards the second language community. I will then briefly
relate these to the distinction between 'instrumental' and 'integrative'
motivation.


### 5.3.1   *Communicative need for a second language*

The primary motive for learning a language is that it provides a means of
communication. A person is therefore most likely to be drawn towards
learning a second language if he perceives a clear communicative need for
it.

The extent of this communicative need depends to a considerable extent on the nature of the social community in which the person lives. For example, in a bilingual or multilingual community, such as Belgium, India or Paraguay, the need for more than one language is apparent in a wide range of social situations. It is also reinforced by the cultural assumptions with which people grow up. A second language is therefore, for many people, simply a normal and necessary extension of their communicative repertoire for coping with life's demands. In this respect, it is a process similar to the acquisition of different styles of speaking, to suit different kinds of situation, in a monolingual community.

There is a similarly transparent need for a second language amongst the linguistic minorities in, for example, many parts of Europe and North America. If an Italian immigrant in West Germany or a Pakistani in Great Britain wishes to develop social contacts or fulfil professional ambitions in the wider society, he must develop an adequate system for communicating with it.

If we wished to make a distinction between 'second' and 'foreign' language learning, the situations just described would be classified as 'second' language learning. This term indicates that the language has communicative functions inside the community where the learner lives. We can compare this with what is often called a 'foreign' language learning situation. This means that the language has no established functions inside the learner's community but will be used mainly for communicating with outsiders. Foreign language learning would thus include the learning of French in Great Britain, the learning of English in Germany or Holland, and so on.

When the language is being used for external rather than internal communication, people are less likely to be sharply or constantly aware of a communicative need for it. For many people, there may be no such awareness at all. For example, many school learners of French in Great Britain have no clear conception of themselves ever using the language for fulfilling real communicative needs, partly because they have little contact with French people and partly because English is itself a world language. We may compare this with the situation of, say, a learner of English in Holland. Because the Dutch-speaking community is small and English provides an important means of communicating outside its boundaries (often with other non-native speakers of the language), this learner is considerably more likely to perceive the communicative value of the foreign language and, as a consequence, to be motivated to acquire proficiency in it.

We have considered the matter of communicative need mainly from a broad community perspective: by their nature, some communities are more likely to produce large numbers of learners motivated by perceived communicative need. However, this global view is not sufficient and we should remember that, inside any community, there is wide variation between individuals. For example, in a linguistic minority, some members will have less desire than others for contact with the wider society. The result may be that they achieve only limited proficiency in the second language, perhaps just enough to satisfy their 'survival' needs. This has been observed in West Germany, for example, amongst some immigrant workers who have strong ambitions to return to their home country. It is also the case with the older women in some immigrant families in Great Britain, especially when the cultural tradition prevents women from having many contacts outside the home.

Conversely, it is obvious that many individual learners in Great Britain perceive a high degree of communicative value in a foreign language and reach an advanced level of proficiency in it. It may be significant in this context that Clare Burstall et al. (1974) found more successful foreign language learners amongst children of middle-class families, which may be more oriented than working-class families towards contacts outside their own community. A major effort is currently being made in British schools to design courses which will encourage all children to perceive a foreign language as a valuable instrument for communication.

## 5.3.2  *Attitudes towards the second language community*

When a learner is favourably disposed towards the speakers of the language he is learning, there are two main reasons why his motivation is likely to benefit.

First, the learner with more favourable attitudes will wish for more intensive contact with the second language community. In this respect, favourable attitudes reinforce the factor discussed in the previous section: the extent to which a learner perceives communicative need. In situations where circumstances do not actually compel members of different language groups to have contact with each other, the learner's attitudes may determine whether he perceives any communicative need at all.

If the first reason concerned mainly the *purpose* of learning a second language, the second reason concerns its *nature*. There is a close link between the way we speak and the way we perceive our identity and our world. When we try to adopt new speech patterns, we are to some extent giving up markers of our own identity in order to adopt those of another cultural group. In some respects, too, we are accepting another culture's ways of perceiving the world. If we are agreeable to this process, it can enrich us and liberate us. If not, it can be a source of resentment and insecurity. One of the factors influencing how we experience the process is our attitude towards the foreign culture itself. If this attitude is negative, there may be strong internal barriers against learning, and if learning has to take place because of external compulsion, it may proceed only to the minimum level required by these external demands.

There are some learning situations where many learners have not had sufficient experience of the second language community to have attitudes for or against it. Again, many learners of French or German in Great Britain provide an example. In cases such as this, it is probable that attitudes relate more directly to learning as it is experienced in the classroom. One important aspect of this experience is the image of the community which the learner derives from the teacher and the materials. If this image remains secondhand, however, it may remain a weak factor compared with more general aspects of motivation, such as enjoyment, stimulation through variety and, above all, the experience of success. It is significant that two major studies of foreign language learners in Great Britain (Burstall et al., 1974; Green, 1975) found no clear evidence that the learners' initial attitudes were an important contributor to their eventual proficiency. However, successful learners developed favourable attitudes as the course progressed, and in their turn, these attitudes encouraged more success. One of Burstall et al.'s most confident conclusions is therefore that, in language learning as in other forms of learning, 'nothing succeeds like success'. The converse of this is, of course, that failure may produce negative attitudes which may help to breed further failure.

There is another type of learning situation in which attitudes to another community may be less decisive in influencing motivation and proficiency. This is when a second language is learnt primarily not for the sake of contact with the native-speaking community, but for communication with others who have learnt it as a second language. English has increasingly taken on this function as an 'international' language in recent decades, serving as a lingua franca either within a multilingual country (such as India) or between people from different countries who do not speak each other's native language (e.g. a former German chancellor and French president – Helmut Schmidt and Giscard d'Estaing – used it to communicate with each other). When English is learned primarily for this international function, we would not expect the learner's attitudes towards native-speaking English communities to exert such an important influence. This expectation is supported by research described in the next section.

### 5.3.3 *Integrative and instrumental motivation*

The effects of attitudes on motivation and proficiency have been investigated in a large number of studies, notably those by Robert Gardner and Wallace Lambert (1972). These researchers have related their findings to two basic kinds of motivation, which they call 'integrative' and 'instrumental'. These are distinguished as follows:

1 A learner with integrative motivation has a genuine interest in the second language community. He wants to learn their language in order to communicate with them more satisfactorily and to gain closer contact with them and their culture.
2 A learner with instrumental motivation is more interested in how the second language can be a useful instrument towards furthering other goals, such as gaining a necessary qualification or improving employment prospects.

The distinction is similar to that made between 'intrinsic' and 'extrinsic' motivation in general learning theory. It is clear that the two kinds of motivation do not exclude each other: most learners are motivated by a mixture of integrative and instrumental reasons.

Gardner and Lambert have studied mainly English-speaking learners of French in areas of North America where there is a community of French native speakers close at hand. Their results from these studies show that learners with a higher *integrative* orientation are likely to achieve greater proficiency. This is what we would expect in the light of the previous discussion: the integrative learner would wish for more social contact and also be happier in adopting new speech patterns from the other group.

However, Gardner and Lambert obtained different results when they studied learners of English in the Philippines. Here, they found the level of the learners' *instrumental* motivation correlated best with their success in second language learning. Yasmeen Lukmani (1972) found the same when she studied learners of English in India. In both of these situations, English is learnt as an international language rather than with reference to a community of English native speakers, so that it is not surprising if integrative attitudes are not so significant as the learner's instrumental reasons for wanting the language.

## 5.4 Opportunities for learning

If we assume now that a learner is well motivated to learn a second language, another important influence on the proficiency he achieves will be the quality of the learning opportunities which the environment offers. Here, we will discuss four aspects of this influence: the opportunities that exist for using the second language, the emotional climate of the learning situations, the type of language to which the learner is exposed (his 'linguistic input'), and the effects of formal instruction.

### 5.4.1 *Opportunities to use the second language*

In chapters 3 and 4, we saw evidence that many aspects of second language acquisition occur through natural learning mechanisms, which are activated when the learner is involved in communicative activity. If this is so, it is important that the learner should have access to situations where the language is used as a natural means of communication.

In some situations, this factor is inseparable from communicative need, as discussed earlier. In a bilingual community, for example, the proximity of another language group may create simultaneously the communicative need for the second language and the opportunites for learning it through use. In other situations, however, the two factors are separate. For example, native English speakers in many parts of Canada or Wales may have no compelling communicative need to learn French or Welsh, but if they do so, the availability of groups of native speakers is a considerable asset. Similarly, learners of French in the south of England have an advantage over their counterparts in the north, because France is within comparatively easy reach.

It is not enough in itself, of course, for learners to simply visit, or even reside in, the other country. It is important, both for learning and for the development of positive attitudes, that they should interact with native speakers at a personal level. This is more likely to occur when the initial attitudes towards contact are favourable and the learner feels confident in the strange environment.

### 5.4.2 *Emotional climate of learning situations*

In an environment where learners feel anxious or insecure, there are likely to be psychological barriers to communication. Also, if anxiety rises above a certain level, it is an obstacle to the learning process. Unfortunately, the two kinds of situation where second language learning takes place most often – the classroom and the second language community – can easily generate situations where learners feel overanxious.

In the typical language classroom, learners are often asked to perform in a state of ignorance and dependence which may engender feelings of helplessness. They have to produce unfamiliar sounds in front of an audience. When they do not perform adequately, they may be subjected to comment and correction, sometimes for reasons that are not clear to them. Most of them do not possess the linguistic tools to express their own individuality. In any case, there is usually little opportunity for this, since the interaction is dominated by the teacher.

In a similar way, the second language environment may cause learners to feel anxious and constrained. With their limited communicative competence, they may have difficulties in relating to others and presenting their own selves adequately. For example, making casual conversation or expressing spontaneous reactions may be difficult, and attempts to do so may result in misunderstandings and laborious efforts to explain. Unless they have firm confidence in themselves, they may come to feel that they project a silly, boring image, and become withdrawn. Their sense of alienation may be increased by the fact that they are having to re-learn the conventions which surround simple daily events, such as eating in a restaurant or approaching an acquaintance. To use two terms commonly applied to this kind of experience: they may develop a sense of 'reduced personality' and experience varying degrees of 'culture shock'.

More fortunate learners may establish friendly contacts in the second language environment, which cushion their relationship with it and make them more willing to expose themselves in the new language. In the classroom, too, a sympathetic teacher and co-operative atmosphere may have a similarly supportive effect. It is significant that current discussions about methodology pay particular attention to creating such situations.

We should remember, however, that the level of anxiety felt by learners is only partly a result of the nature of the situation itself. It is also a result of personal factors. For example, some learners become anxious more quickly than others, whatever the situation. Others may have had experiences of failure which cause them to become anxious quickly in classroom learning situations.

We should also note that psychological research suggests that, at least in formal learning situations, we should not necessarily feel obliged to eliminate anxiety altogether. Whereas too much anxiety hinders learning, it seems that a certain amount of it can stimulate a learner to invest more energy in the task. However, the optimal level depends on various factors, such as the learner's ability or the nature of the learning task.

### 5.4.3 *The nature of the linguistic input*

We saw in the first chapter (section 1.8) how the speech which people address to children usually differs from that which they address to adults. For example, it is typically simpler in structure and more limited in vocabulary, contains more repetition, and is more closely related to the immediate situation. The language is therefore easier to understand and the child has more opportunity to organise it and remember it. Many researchers believe that these features play an important role in helping first language acquisition to take place.

Similarly, it seems probable that the nature of the speech addressed to *second* language learners is an important factor in influencing how well they learn. Indeed, it is now often proposed that the ideal input for acquiring a second language is similar to the input received by the child: comprehensible, relevant to their immediate interests, not too complex but not strictly graded, either. Exposed to this kind of input, the learner's natural acquisition mechanisms can operate, picking out the structures for which they are ready at any given time. This could explain why children are often more successful than adults in natural learning situations: because their minds are simpler and more oriented towards the here-and-now, they are exposed to speech which is likewise simpler, more related to concrete matters, and therefore more comprehensible. Adults, on the other hand, are often expected to understand speech which is more complex and less concrete.

As I said earlier (section 5.2), practical difficulties mean that nobody has actually tested the effects of different kinds of input on second language learning. Information about this would obviously be of crucial value for improving teaching. Most teaching approaches to date have been based on the assumption that the learner's input should be carefully controlled and graded for structural complexity. However, it is now sometimes suggested that this assumption is mistaken, and that classrooms should concentrate on providing the kind of input described above: comprehensible, interesting, relevant, but not strictly graded. We will return to this idea in the next chapter (section 6.2) and in chapter 8 (section 8.4).

### 5.4.4  *The effects of formal instruction*

It is clear from the studies described in chapter 4 that, given the right kinds of natural exposure, formal instruction is not necessary for second language learning. We now need to consider to what extent – and in what ways – it *helps* learning.

In formal instruction, teachers attempt to affect the course of learning, mainly by such means as: controlling the learner's exposure to the language; making them become aware of significant features and patterns; providing opportunities for practising the language; ensuring that learners receive feedback about their performance. Within this general framework, an immense variety of teaching approaches is possible, and it is obvious that some teachers have developed more successful approaches than others. However, it is not at all clear what factors determine their success.

There have been a number of studies comparing the effectiveness of different methodologies, such as grammar–translation or audio-lingual methods. These have been inconclusive, probably because no single methodology is intrinsically 'better' than others in all situations. Also, attempts to make fair comparisons are hindered by the fact that results are influenced by such a vast number of factors not related to the methodology as such. These include the personality and skill of individual teachers, the ability and motivation of different learning groups, the availability of time and resources, and so on. In fact, one of the clearest conclusions to emerge is that, at least in the present state of our knowledge about possible methodologies, these other factors together play a more significant role than the choice between one methodology and another.

There have also been attempts to investigate the effectiveness not of complete methodologies, but of specific techniques. These have shed some light on pedagogical factors which might influence success for particular groups of learners, though their findings have been suggestive rather than conclusive. Thus the large-scale study of Clare Burstall et al. (1974), with young children learning French in Great Britain, suggested that these learners made better progress when they had teachers who used a lot of French in the classroom (but without confusing them), did not rely too much on mechanical repetition, and provided visual stimuli. The GUME project in Sweden (see Levin, 1972) found that most adolescents and adults learnt better when practice with drills was preceded by an explanation of the structure involved. Valerian Postovsky (1974) found that adults became more proficient when they were not required to produce the language orally during the first four weeks of their course.

If a person has ample opportunities for informal learning, to what extent does formal instruction help at all? Of the studies which have examined this question, some have found, as one might expect, that learners who have received more formal instruction are also more proficient. However, some studies have found little or no relationship between instruction and proficiency. For example, Ann Fathman (1975) studied children aged between six and fifteen learning English in the United States. She concluded that proficiency did not seem to depend on whether their school provided formal instruction in English. John Upshur (1968) reached a similar conclusion about adult students whom he tested. Results such as this have led some people (notably Stephen Krashen) to argue that formal instruction is only a crucial factor when it is the learner's sole or major source of language experience. When the learner also has ample opportunity for natural acquisition through communicative use, its role may be comparatively insignificant. Perhaps future research will cast more light on this question.

We cannot always make a sharp distinction between natural learning and learning in the classroom. As work on error analysis makes clear (c.f. chapter 3), the learner's natural processes are active inside the classroom as well as outside. In another study, involving school learners of English in Germany, Sascha Felix (1981) found that many of the learners' utterances reflected the natural developmental sequences described in chapter 4, rather than the forms which had been presented and drilled by the teacher. Increasingly, teachers are now attempting to exploit these natural processes rather than combat them, by providing communicative experience in the classroom which is as similar as possible to communication in the natural environment. The more realistic this classroom communication becomes and the more frequently it takes place, the more blurred becomes the distinction between natural and formal learning.

## 5.5 Ability to learn

So far in this chapter, we have looked at two sets of factors which influence how successful a person is in learning a second language: the nature of the person's *motivation* to learn and the qualities of the *opportunities* to learn. We now turn to a third set of factors: those which make up the person's *ability* to learn.

Here I propose to use 'ability' in a broader sense than is often the case. The term is often restricted to cognitive aspects of a person's ability to learn, notably intelligence and a set of more specific language-learning abilities called 'language aptitude'. Here, I will use it to refer to a broader set of factors which – given similar motivation and opportunities – make some people better at learning than others. In particular, I will take it to include not only cognitive factors, but also the effects of personality, age, and active strategies which the learner adopts.

### 5.5.1 *Cognitive factors*

There is a link between general intelligence ('IQ') and second-language-learning ability. This was found, for example, by Gardner and Lambert in the studies described earlier (5.3.3). As a further example, Paul Pimsleur (1968) found that a school learner's average grades in all school subjects were often a good means of predicting how good he would be at language learning. Pimsleur therefore included these grades in his battery of tests for language aptitude.

However, it has also become clear that success in second language learning is related not only to general cognitive ability, but also to a more language-specific set of learning abilities which are usually called 'language aptitude'. Language aptitude is a phenomenon whose exact nature is not yet known. It has been investigated most intensively by researchers attempting to devise tests of students' learning potential before they actually begin a course. One of the best known of these tests, the 'Modern Language Aptitude Test' of John Carroll and Stanley Sapon (1959), focusses on the following abilities, in the belief that they form part of language aptitude:

1 the ability to identify and remember sounds;
2 the ability to memorise words;

3 the ability to recognise how words function grammatically in sentences;
4 the ability to induce grammatical rules from language examples.

The 'Language Aptitude Battery' of Pimsleur includes tests of similar abilities.

As we might expect, intelligence and language aptitude have generally been found to correlate best with the more 'academic' language skills which are often stressed at school, such as reading or performing in grammar-manipulation tests (see e.g. Genesee, 1976). Attitudes and motivation, on the other hand, seem to be linked especially with the ability to use language for interpersonal communication.

Taken together, language aptitude and motivation (based on favourable attitudes) are the factors which have predicted success most regularly in the various research studies. Nonetheless, there is still a lot of variation between learners that these factors do not explain. As an illustration, Gardner (1980) analysed results from twenty-nine groups of Canadian learners of French. He found that their scores on his 'Attitude-Motivation Index' accounted, on average, for 14 per cent of the variation in proficiency. Their results on the Modern Language Aptitude Test accounted for 17 per cent. By combining the scores for both attitude-motivation and aptitude, Gardner could account for 27 per cent of the variation. In other words, there was still 73 per cent of the variation in learners' success that was due to other factors – including, presumably, the other factors discussed in this chapter. However, we should remember the point made in section 5.2 above: the accuracy of these results depends on the validity of the tests, so that the actual contribution of aptitude and motivation to learning could be greater.

There have been other suggestions for cognitive factors which may influence success in language learning. For example, since learners have to make suitable generalisations about the language, it seems plausible that one such factor could be a person's strategies in categorising experience. Neil Naiman et al. (1978) therefore examined whether success was linked to 'category width' – that is, whether a person tends to form broad or narrow categories. They found no significant link. They did, however, find that proficiency (in listening and imitating sentences) seemed to be related to 'field independence' – that is, being able to perceive individual items without being distracted by background material. Perhaps this ability helps the learner to perceive relevant items and patterns in the stream of language to which he is exposed.

Some cognitive differences may dispose learners to particular *kinds* of learning and thus place them at an advantage, or disadvantage, in certain kinds of course. For example, some people seem to rely more than others on a visual stimulus, and might be more successful in a course where the written word is prominent. Another significant difference might be whether a person is happier learning 'deductively' (proceeding from rules to examples) or 'inductively' (discovering rules from examples).

It seems reasonable to assume that second language learning must be influenced by many other cognitive factors than those mentioned here. Our knowledge in this area is still very limited and we must hope that future research will extend it.

### 5.5.2 *Personality*

As with cognitive factors, a number of personality characteristics have been proposed as likely to influence second language learning. These proposals are often supported by observation or intuition, but it has not proved easy to demonstrate them in empirical studies. This could mean that the links between personality and second-language-learning ability are weaker than had been supposed. However, in view of the problem involved in measuring personality traits in a reliable way, it is equally likely that the tests are not providing reliable information.

It is often suggested that an *extrovert* person is especially well suited to second language learning. However, when Naiman et al. investigated whether good language learners scored higher in a standard test of extroversion, their results were negative. A more positive result emerged from a study by Richard Tucker et al. (1976), who found that success in second language learning seemed to correlate with learners' scores on some traits often associated with extroversion, such as assertiveness and adventuresomeness.

We might note here that irrespective of actual learning ability, people with an outgoing personality may enjoy certain advantages. For example, they may become involved in more social interaction, attract more attention from their teachers, and be less inhibited when asked to display their proficiency (e.g. in oral interviews). They may perform more confidently in communication situations, whichever language they are using.

A study by Adelaide Heyde (1979) found that a high level of *self-esteem* was associated with second language proficiency. Presumably, learners with high self-esteem are less likely to feel threatened when communicating in a strange language or in an unfamiliar situation (c.f. section 5.4.2). They may also be more ready to risk making mistakes or projecting a reduced image of themselves.

Naiman et al. found that learners with greater *tolerance for ambiguity* scored higher in tests of listening comprehension. Presumably, if learners can tolerate uncertainty without feeling insecure or confused, they are less likely to feel overwhelmed by the large amounts of strange material they must face when learning a second language.

Finally, there is some evidence, from studies by Alexander Guiora et al.

(1975), that learners with a high capacity for *empathy* (that is, appreci-
ating other people's thoughts and feelings) may perform better in at least
one aspect of a second language: pronunciation. Since the way that a
person speaks is closely associated with his sense of identity (c.f. section
5.3.2), it may be that empathy helps a learner to step outside his present
identity in order to adopt new patterns of behaviour.

Despite the largely inconclusive results so far, many people believe that
personality will one day be shown to be an important influence on success
in second language learning. The relationship may not be a simple one,
however. It is more likely that personality interacts in complex ways with
other factors in order to affect learning. As purely speculative examples:
extroversion could turn out to be a greater advantage in natural learning
situations than in formal learning, or when it is combined with a high
degree of field independence. Similarly, of course, particular *combinations* of personality traits may be important, rather than particular traits
in themselves.

### 5.5.3 *Age*

For many people, it is almost axiomatic that children can learn a second
language better than adults. They refer especially to immigrant families
where children have learnt the language of their new community with
native or near-native proficiency, whereas the adults always show traces
of foreignness. Also, studies of immigrants to North America (e.g.
Ramsey and Wright, 1974) and West Germany (e.g. Klein and Dittmar,
1979) provide concrete evidence that the younger a person is on arrival in
the new country, the more proficient he or she is likely to become in the
language.

The most common explanation for these observations is that there is a
'critical period', during which the brain is flexible and language learning
can occur naturally and easily. Since this period ends around puberty,
adolescents and adults can no longer call upon these natural learning
capacities. The result is that language learning becomes an artificial,
laborious process.

However, this account has been criticised in recent years, from a
number of standpoints. From a biological standpoint, people have ques-
tioned whether there is any real evidence that puberty is accompanied by
changes in the brain that are so crucial to language learning. Experience
shows, too, that many adolescents and adults do acquire a high level of
proficiency in a second language, which would scarcely be possible if they
lacked important learning mechanisms. The existence of these mechanisms is also confirmed by studies such as those described in chapters 3 and
4, which provide strong evidence that older learners have not lost their
capacities for natural language learning.

One difficulty in comparing the learning ability of children and older learners is that, in the majority of cases, children have better learning conditions than older learners: more time, attention, communicative need, opportunities for use, and so on. In an attempt to make a fairer comparison, some researchers have studied situations where the opportunities for learning are similar for learners of different ages. In many cases, they have found that older learners seem to learn more efficiently. In Holland, for example, Catherine Snow and Marian Hoefnagel-Höhle (1978) found that English-speaking adolescents acquired Dutch more quickly than younger children. In America, Ann Fathman (1975) found that learners of English aged between eleven and fifteen acquired grammar (but not pronunciation) more quickly than children aged between six and ten. These studies involved learners with large amounts of natural exposure. Similar results with school learners have emerged from other studies, notably that of Clare Burstall et al. (1974) in Great Britain. Indeed, the weight of evidence suggests that, given more or less equal opportunities, efficiency in second language learning increases with age, and that younger learners are superior only in acquiring pronunciation skills.

If it is true that efficiency increases with age, how can one account for the common observation that immigrant children are often quicker than their parents at learning a new language? We can, in fact, find possible explanations in terms of some of the other factors discussed in this chapter, for example:

1 As I indicated above, children often have more favourable learning conditions. They are often exposed to the language for longer periods of time and receive more intensive attention from native speakers of the language, including other children.
2 They are likely to be exposed to simpler language, which is easier to process and understand, both from adults and from other children.
3 They are less likely to hold negative attitudes towards other speech communities or to be aware of other factors (e.g. fear of rejection) which may produce barriers to interaction and learning.
4 The adult's tendency to analyse and apply conscious thought to the learning experience may obstruct some of the natural processing mechanisms through which the new language is internalised. In terms of a distinction which some researchers make and which will be discussed in more detail in the next chapter (c.f. section 6.4): it may be that older learners rely too much on 'learning', whereas children are content to let 'acquisition' take its proper course.

Because fewer people now believe that children are intrinsically superior to adults in second language learning, there has recently been a decline in support for the movements in several countries to introduce it into schools at an early age (e.g. seven or eight).

### 5.5.4   Active learning strategies

There are a number of active strategies which people might adopt in order to learn more effectively. Researchers have recently observed and interviewed classroom learners, in an attempt to discover which of these strategies seem to be most helpful. The clearest results have emerged from studies in Canada, by Neil Naiman et al. (1978) and by Marjorie Wesche (1979).

From these studies, it seems that successful language learners employ a wide variety of strategies which demonstrate, above all, their active involvement in learning. For example, they may repeat silently to themselves the sounds they hear from the teacher or other students. When the teacher puts a question to another student, they often think out their own answer and compare it with the answer accepted by the teacher. When learning or producing dialogues, they make efforts to identify with their foreign language roles and to pay close attention to the meaning of the language they are using. They are likely to take opportunities to discuss the lesson material with other students. Outside the classroom, they exploit every opportunity to use the language as a means of communication, for example by seeking personal contacts, listening to the radio, or reading newspapers.

Some observational studies of successful second language learners through natural exposure suggest that they, too, benefit from developing active strategies. In particular, they find ways to increase the scope for social interaction. For example, Evelyn Hatch (1978c) suggests that they develop techniques for keeping the conversation flowing smoothly. Lily Wong-Fillmore (1976) notes that a common strategy among child learners is to attach themselves to a group of other children and pretend to understand, even when they probably do not.

## 5.6   Conclusion

In this chapter, we have looked at some of the factors which might help to explain why some second language learners are more successful than others. I have classified these factors according to whether they relate primarily to the learners' motivation, their opportunities for learning, or their ability to learn.

A useful alternative way of classifying these same factors is according to whether they are internal or external to the learner. Ability factors are internal to the learner whereas opportunities depend largely on what the external environment provides. Motivation results from an interplay between internal and external factors. The main practical significance of this alternative classification is that external factors can often be directly manipulated in order to help learning (e.g. by providing certain kinds of input, arranging trips to the other country, and so on). Internal factors can sometimes be influenced in a less direct way (e.g. teaching about the country may create more favourable attitudes), but it is more often a question of having to simply recognise them and take account of them as much as possible (e.g. by modifying courses to suit different levels of aptitude).

From time to time, I have pointed out that the various factors must interact in complex ways to affect second language learning. We still do not know much about these complex ways. Indeed, the sum of our knowledge about the factors influencing second language learning is very limited and imprecise. We are still a long way from being able to predict, with any degree of reliability, how successfully a specific individual will learn. We are equally far away from being able to modify the external factors (e.g. through teaching) with any confidence that we are really providing the best possible conditions for learning. Therefore, our explorations must continue.

# 6 Models of second language learning

## 6.1 Introduction

We have now discussed the processes by which second languages are learnt (chapters 2, 3 and 4), the sequences in which they are learnt (notably chapter 4) and some of the factors which influence how well they are learnt (chapter 5). In the present chapter, we will look at some conceptual frameworks (or 'models') which might help us to relate these various elements to each other and enable us to form a coherent picture of the nature and causes of second language learning.

In the sections which now follow, we will discuss various aspects of the 'creative construction' model, which has already been referred to at several points in the book. Then, we will move to a model which seems, at first sight, to present a conflicting view: the 'skill-learning' model. It is this model that underlies most teaching. Finally, we will consider how the models may be reconciled and integrated into one account.

## 6.2 Second language learning as creative construction

As we have seen in previous chapters, a model of second language learning that has become increasingly influential is one which sees it as a process of 'creative construction'. According to this model, a learner 'constructs' a series of internal representations of the second language system. This occurs as a result of natural processing strategies and exposure to the second language in communication situations. Provided the right kind of exposure takes place, the learner's internal representations develop gradually, in predictable stages, in the direction of the native speaker's competence. We saw this especially in chapter 4, in connection with the learning of some morphemes and grammatical constructions of English and German.

This model owes a lot to similar ones proposed for first language learning. Diagrammatically, we can represent it as follows:

Second     Natural     Temporary
language $\rightarrow$ processing $\rightarrow$ representation $\rightarrow$ Utterances
exposure     strategies    of the system

Most of the concrete evidence for this model comes from inspecting the last item in the diagram: the learners' utterances. In chapters 3 and 4, we saw a number of studies which have done this, by either focussing on learners' errors or examining all utterances containing a particular item. These utterances enable us to draw conclusions about the kind of system which the learners have internalised (e.g. their rules for forming negatives or interrogatives). Moving a further step back from the actual utterances, we can hypothesise about the processing strategies which might lead learners to form these rules on the basis of their exposure to the language. As we also saw in chapters 3 and 4, important strategies seem to be generalisation, transfer, redundancy reduction and imitation. The kind of second language input on which these strategies can operate most effectively may share some of the features associated with adults' talk to children, notably its focus on clear and relevant communication (c.f. chapter 5, section 5.4.3).

A notable feature of the creative construction model, in the form just presented, is that the internal processing mechanisms operate on the input from the language environment and are not directly dependent on the learners' attempts to produce the language themselves. The learners' own utterances are a natural outcome of the system they have internalised, rather than a factor contributing to the process of internalisation. As evidence for this, reference is made especially to the 'silent period' which occurs in the early stages of first language learning and natural second language learning, and which has also been successfully introduced into second language teaching programmes (e.g. by Valerian Postovsky). However, learners' utterances still play an important indirect role, since they enable learners to take part in communication situations and thus to gain more input. We may also argue that learners process many items more intensively because of the prospective need to produce them in their own speech, particularly if these items are redundant to immediate comprehension needs.

We shall see that one of the chief differences between the creative construction model and the skill-learning model (c.f. section 6.3) lies in the role they attribute to the learner's own attempts to produce the language.

## 6.2.1 *Second language learning as 'acculturation'*

Language is a means of communication and, as we saw in chapter 5 (section 5.3), a major factor in accounting for varying success in second language learning is the extent to which it is motivated by real communicative needs. These needs may be of two main kinds:
(a) *functional* needs: the desire to convey messages without misunderstanding, to carry out transactions efficiently, and so on;

(b) *social* needs: the desire to use language which is socially acceptable and enables the learner to integrate satisfactorily with the second language community.

These two kinds of need overlap considerably and we should not attempt to draw too sharp a distinction. However, to some extent we can distinguish between learners who are only interested in the functional (e.g. 'survival') value of the second language, and those who are also interested in becoming integrated socially with the other community. It is this difference in emphasis that underlies the concepts of 'instrumental' and 'integrative' motivation (c.f. 5.3.3).

The idea that learners differ in the degree to which they aim for integration with the other community forms the basis of the 'acculturation' hypothesis for second language learning. This is best seen not as an alternative to the creative construction model, but as complementary to it. It focusses not so much on the actual processing of the second language as on the social and psychological conditions under which this processing is most likely to take place successfully. It states simply that the more a person aspires to be integrated with the other community, the further he will progress along the developmental continuum.

Concrete evidence for this hypothesis comes mainly from studies in America (see Schumann, 1976b, 1978b; Stauble, 1980) and West Germany (see Dittmar and Klein, 1979; Meisel et al., 1981). Schumann found, for example, that despite ample learning opportunities, one adult learner did not progress beyond the early stages in acquiring English structures. Interviews and questionnaires showed that this learner was socially distant from the English-speaking community and had little desire for integration. The other studies found similar links between the learners' desire for social contact and their progress along the developmental continuum.

The main contribution of the acculturation hypothesis is that it helps to explain the motivational factors which cause the creative construction process to take place. In particular, it illuminates the nature of the communicative needs which provide the dynamism for the process, by emphasising that these needs exist at a deep psychological level as well as at a superficial transactional level.

## 6.2.2   *Second language learning as the elaboration of a 'simple code'*

In its earliest stages, the speech produced by second language learners shows a marked resemblance not only to the early speech of children (c.f. chapters 1 and 4), but also to pidgins. These are all 'reduced systems', or 'simple codes', which share features such as the following:

1 Many of their linguistic characteristics are the same. For example, redundant inflections and function words (e.g. prepositions) tend to be omitted; meaning is signalled above all by word order; complex grammatical constructions are avoided; and the vocabulary is reduced.

2 In each case, the reduced system satisfies a correspondingly reduced range of communicative needs. These are mainly simple functional needs, since the system lacks the fine distinctions which would transmit subtle concepts or social meanings.

3 As the speakers' needs become more complex or subtle, the system becomes more elaborate. Thus, the first or second language learner moves through developmental sequences such as those described in chapters 1 and 4. If a pidgin becomes established as a social group's primary language, it will develop into a creole.

It seems, then, that human beings adopt similar kinds of system when they are compelled to communicate with each other in the simplest way available and with limited resources. An attractive hypothesis is that these systems reflect some kind of universal linguistic base, which everybody possesses before language learning begins and which remains available as a basis for later language learning or for rudimentary communication. We saw evidence for some such universal base in chapter 1 (sections 1.4 and 1.5.1), when we noted how first language learners of different communities seem to produce similar kinds of utterances in the initial stages of development. The child elaborates this base into the language of his or her own community. Pidgin speakers may resort to it when they have to devise a means for communicating without knowing each other's language. Second language learners, too, may return to it, as a preliminary to beginning to construct the system of the new language with which they are confronted. This base, together with the initial contact with the second language, may enable the learners to construct their first 'simple code' in the new language, which they can then proceed to elaborate through the process of creative construction already discussed.

As with the acculturation hypothesis, the idea of a universal base is not an alternative to the creative construction model, but is complementary to it. The kernel of the learning model is still creative construction through processes such as generalisation and transfer. The acculturation view is concerned with the conditions in which creative construction is most likely to take place effectively; the idea of a universal basic system is a hypothesis about the starting point for the creative construction process. This is clear from the following formulation by Pit Corder. Provided we take 'communicative needs' to include the learner's desire to integrate, the quotation is also a convenient summary of the point which the present discussion has now reached:

The model of the learning process that emerges is one in which the learner starts his learning programme from a basic, possibly universal grammar which he proceeds to elaborate in response to his exposure to the data of the target language and his communicative needs. The elaboration follows a more or less constant sequence for all learners of a particular language but any particular learner's progress along the developmental continuum is significantly affected by the degree to which his existing knowledge of language may facilitate his advance. (1981, p. 102)

The last part of the quotation is a strong statement that second language development may be helped by transfer from the mother tongue and that the extent of this help depends on how closely the two languages are related.

## 6.3   Second language learning as a form of skill learning

The creative construction model, with which this chapter has been concerned so far, emphasises the cognitive processing strategies that the learners bring to the task, in order to develop internal representations of the second language. It aims above all to explain how learners acquire an underlying knowledge of the language which is independent of actual performance skills. Within the terms of this model, a person can learn a language without ever having to use it productively. Productive skills, when they emerge, are simply the external expression of the system which the learner has internalised at a particular stage of development.

This contrasts sharply with the learning model which is implicit in most current approaches to *teaching* a second language. Most teaching approaches are based on the assumption that if we require learners to produce predetermined pieces of language (e.g. through drills or question-and-answer practice), this productive activity will lead them to internalise the system underlying the language, to the point where they can operate the system without conscious reflection.

Diagrammatically, these differences could be presented as follows:

*Creative construction model:*

| Input from exposure | $\rightarrow$ | Internal processing | $\rightarrow$ | System constructed by learners | $\rightarrow$ | Spontaneous utterances |
|---|---|---|---|---|---|---|

*Model underlying most teaching:*

| Input from instruction | $\rightarrow$ | Productive activity | $\rightarrow$ | System assimilated by learners | $\rightarrow$ | Spontaneous utterances |
|---|---|---|---|---|---|---|

In addition to (a) the different role which the second of these models accords to productive activity, we should also note that (b) the input in this model includes the presentation of controlled samples of the language, together with guidance as to the system which underlies them, and that (c) the system which the learners are expected to internalise is not one which they construct themselves, but the correct native-speaker system which is imposed from outside in a graded sequence. (However, as we saw in chapter 3, learners may still engage in their own process of creative construction, determined by their 'internal' syllabus rather than the external one.)

Unlike the creative construction model, the model which we have now begun to discuss emphasises that the use of a second language is a performance skill. As with other kinds of performance skill, it has a cognitive aspect and a behavioural aspect. The *cognitive* aspect involves the internalisation of plans for creating appropriate behaviour. For language use, these plans derive mainly from the language system – they include grammatical rules, procedures for selecting vocabulary, and social conventions governing speech. The *behavioural* aspect involves the automation of these plans so that they can be converted into fluent performance in real time. This occurs mainly through *practice* in converting plans into performance, i.e. through productive language activity, with receptive activity playing a less clearly defined role.

When a skill is being learned, component parts of the target performance may be isolated and practised separately. In language learning, for example, a learner may practise using a grammatical structure such as the negative, expressing a communicative function such as asking for permission, or producing a phonetic distinction such as that between *ship* and *sheep*. These are instances of 'part-skill practice'. At other times, the total skill may be practised, requiring the component parts to be integrated during performance. For example, the language learner may have to take part in a conversation or write a letter. These are instances of 'whole-task practice'. Of course, there is a wide range of possible levels of difficulty within both part-skill and whole-task practice.

This division into part-skills is possible because of the *hierarchical* nature of language use. That is, using language involves performing tasks, each of which is composed of sub-tasks, each of which is composed of sub-sub-tasks, and so on. For example:

1 At the highest level in the hierarchy, we may have an overall communicative goal. Let us say that we want to persuade a friend to come to see a film this evening.
2 To achieve this goal, we may develop a strategy which consists of various components, such as: state that the film is being shown, indicate what it is about, explain why it would appeal to the friend, argue why this evening would be a suitable time to see it. Some aspects of the strategy might be worked out in advance, others as the conversation proceeds.

3 To carry out each of the sub-tasks just mentioned, we must decide on specific topics (e.g. what arguments to present) and select syntactic patterns.
4 Each syntactic pattern requires operations at the levels of clause, then phrase, then word selection. In other words, using the grammar can itself be seen as involving a hierarchy of tasks.
5 The articulation of the words requires a complex set of motor skills.

Each of the tasks (or sub-tasks, etc.) mentioned above requires a plan for its performance. At the higher levels in the hierarchy (e.g. deciding on strategies or meanings), these plans will probably be composed consciously in the light of the speaker's immediate communicative intentions. However, at the lower levels (e.g. selecting and producing grammatical structures and words to perform these intentions), the competent speaker has ready-made plans available in long-term memory. During performance, therefore, he can devote most of his limited store of attentional capacity to the higher-level tasks and leave the lower-level operations to unfold automatically, in response to higher-level decisions.

Clearly, a person who is still acquiring language skills does not yet possess such a wide repertoire of ready-made, automated plans as the competent speaker. He may therefore find that he has to devote conscious attention to lower-level operations. If he can still carry out the operations correctly, the result may merely be some sacrifice of fluency. However, if he lacks the necessary information or attentional capacity to compose the appropriate plans, the result will be error, for example:

– a *transfer* error, which indicates that the speaker has wrongly activated a plan from his mother-tongue store;
– an *overgeneralisation* error, which indicates that the speaker has activated an inappropriate plan from within the second language system.

As the learner acquires more information and increases his ability to carry out lower-level operations automatically, the accuracy and fluency of the performance will improve. This process is described by Willem Levelt as follows:

The acquisition of skill consists essentially of automation of low-level plans or units of activity. Initially the execution of such a unit of activity requires the allocation of a large amount of mental effort, since it has to be designed anew (like constructing an actual negative sentence in French from knowledge of the rules of negation). Repeated performance of the activity, however, leads to the availability of ready-made plans in long-term memory for such activities . . . The result of automation is that less and less effort is to be spent on lower-level patterns of action, so that more and more capacity is left for the higher-level decisions.   (1978, pp. 57–8)

At this point, it is interesting to place Levelt's summary of the skill-learning model by the side of Corder's formulation of the creative construction model, quoted at the end of section 6.2.2. The differences are striking, yet they both describe models of second language learning which have appeal for teachers and researchers, on the grounds of experience and intuition. This means that, unless we wish to conclude that one of the models is simply to be rejected, we must look for a way of reconciling them. We will consider this problem in the next sections.

## 6.4 Subconscious and conscious aspects of second language learning

The creative construction model and the skill-learning model make similar assumptions about the goal of language learning. Learners should eventually possess a set of cognitive structures (which we can call 'rules' or 'plans') by means of which they can create language purposefully but flexibly, in response to their communicative intentions. However, the two models envisage different routes to this goal. In creative construction, learning consists of the global (rather than piece-meal) elaboration of an internal system, whose individual parts are integrated with each other from the outset. This development occurs spontaneously and subconsciously, while the learner's attention is on other matters. In the skill-learning model, on the other hand, the dominant form of learning is the step-by-step assimilation of individual parts of the system, which eventually become integrated with each other. This development is susceptible to conscious guidance and training.

To a large degree, then, the two models draw attention to two different kinds of learning: on the one hand, learning which occurs subconsciously, and on the other hand, learning which occurs through conscious effort. The distinction between these two kinds of learning is a familiar one in the psychology of learning. It is reflected in contrasts such as that between 'informal' and 'formal' learning, 'spontaneous' and 'controlled' learning, or 'natural' and 'didactic' learning environments. In language teaching, the distinction is also familiar. More than sixty years ago, for example, Harold Palmer (1922) wrote about the need to utilise both our 'spontaneous' and our 'studial' capacities for language learning. More recently, Stephen Krashen (e.g. 1981a, 1982) and many others have discussed the distinction and its implications. There has, of course, been a considerable increase of interest in the subconscious aspects of language learning, as a result of studies such as those discussed in chapters 3 and 4.

In current discussions, the term 'acquisition' is often used for the subconscious aspects of learning, while the term 'learning' is reserved for the conscious aspects. For the rest of the present chapter, it will be convenient to adopt the same terminology.

In the present state of our knowledge, we cannot make precise or reliable statements about the relationship between acquisition and learning or about the contribution which each makes to a person's ability in a second language. A number of possibilities have been proposed, including the following:

1 One theory (proposed by Krashen) is that acquisition and learning feed into separate systems which perform different functions. During communicative language use (as opposed to, say, conscious language exercises), it is the acquired system that is used to create spontaneous utterances. The learned system acts only as a 'monitor' to improve the formal correctness of the language. However, it can only perform this function if there is sufficient time. This would explain why learners often produce structures correctly when there is no time-pressure, but produce deviant forms when they have to communicate spontaneously.

   However, there is no clear evidence that the two systems remain separate, and many researchers consider this unlikely in the light of what we know about cognitive processes in general.

2 Another account (supported, for example, by Earl Stevick, 1980) agrees that acquisition and learning represent different ways of internalising language. However, it argues that the acquired and learned systems do not remain separate, but can 'bleed' into one another. If we take our main framework as creative construction, this would mean that as a result of practice, structures which have been consciously learnt could pass into the acquired store. They would then become available for use in spontaneous language activity, together with the structures acquired through creative construction.

3 Within the skill-learning framework, we could propose that there are two ways for automated structures (or 'plans') to develop. One is through conscious learning and practice. The other is for them to develop spontaneously through natural processes of acquisition. Thus, as Kari Sajavaara (1978) has suggested, acquisition could be seen as the development, in predictable sequences, of plans that are already automated when they emerge, and can operate without conscious attention. In communicative language use, there would be an intermingling of plans developed via acquisition and learning. However, learned plans which have not yet become automated could not be utilised to full effect except under conditions where the speaker has spare attentional capacity to devote to them.

The second and third of the accounts just presented differ mainly in emphasis. The second takes creative construction as the basic framework and accommodates skill learning within it. The third takes the skill-learning model as its basic framework and accommodates creative construction within it. It may be that each of these accounts has equal potential as a way of representing our experience and intuitions. If so, our choice may depend not so much on the intrinsic adequacy of each account as on the type of learning environment we are most interested in: a 'natural' environment in which creative construction processes are likely to dominate, or a 'didactic' environment in which we might expect conscious learning and practice to play a greater role.

## 6.5 Second language learning as a form of social learning

Another potentially useful way of integrating the two models of learning into a single framework is to place them into a broader learning model which can embrace them both as complementary aspects of human development. In the present section, we will look at creative construction and skill learning from the perspective of social learning theory.

According to recent work in social learning, learning depends on the following basic conditions:

1 motivation to learn;
2 internal representation of the crucial features of the behaviour to be learned;
3 practice in converting this internal representation into actual performance;
4 feedback about the success of the resulting behaviour.

We can see how these basic conditions are fulfilled in different ways in creative construction and skill learning:

MOTIVATION TO LEARN

1 For creative construction to take place, motivation must probably be based on communicative need for the second language. The need may be immediate or longer-term.
2 In skill learning, it may also be due to factors related directly to the context of instruction, such as short-term behavioural objectives, which have little to do with communication as such.

INTERNAL REPRESENTATION OF CRUCIAL FEATURES

1 In creative construction, the features to be internalised are discovered by the learners themselves, from the language environment around them. The internalisation process is one of natural 'acquisition'.
2 In skill learning, learners are usually instructed as to the crucial

features which they have to internalise. The internalisation process is subject to attempts to control it through training procedures.

PRACTICE IN CONVERTING INTERNAL REPRESENTATION INTO PERFORMANCE

1 Creative construction takes place most successfully in communication situations where practice is free from artificial constraints. It is controlled only by the meanings which learners wish to communicate and the linguistic resources at their disposal.
2 In the skill-learning framework, practice is often controlled externally, in the light of specific linguistic objectives. As well as practice in the communicative use of the language ('whole-task practice'), there is often practice of separate parts of the language system ('part-skill practice').

FEEDBACK ABOUT SUCCESS

Here, the important factor is the kind of feedback which the learner attends to and perceives as relevant to his own performance goals.

1 For creative construction to take place, the most important feedback relates to how successfully communication has taken place. The learner needs to refine his language competence in order to communicate more effectively or appropriately.
2 In skill learning, the feedback may also relate to the communication of meanings. However, another common kind of feedback is concerned more with the formal aspects of the language produced by learners, especially its degree of correctness.

Social learning theory thus provides us with a perspective for seeing the different kinds of learning that might lead to language ability. It leaves open, of course, the question which we discussed in the previous section: how these different kinds of learning relate to each other and what functions they perform in contributing to communicative language ability.

## 6.6 Conclusion

In this chapter, we have looked at ways of conceptualising second language learning and understanding its nature and causes. First, we dealt with creative construction and skill learning as alternative models of second language learning. Then, we discussed how these two models might be integrated, either by viewing one from the perspective of the other, or by placing them both within a broader framework based on social learning theory.

To conclude, I should stress that to view the problem in terms of two different or contrasting kinds of learning is a simplification which, however useful, may also be misleading. Between the most subconscious processes of 'acquisition' at one extreme and the most conscious forms of 'learning' at the other, it would probably be more realistic to think in terms of a continuum, in which subconscious and conscious processes are mingled to varying degrees. As research continues, we may hope to gain more detailed and reliable knowledge about how these and other processes interact with each other, in the development and use of second language ability. For the present, our knowledge about what actually occurs at the psychological level is very limited, and we must be content with accounts which are both simplified and tentative.

# 7 Using a second language

## 7.1 Introduction

Before we consider, in chapter 8, some implications which the studies and ideas discussed in this book might have for teaching, I propose to digress briefly from the theme of second language development, to look at how learners use their second language competence in order to communicate. First, we will look at some studies which show how the speech of second language learners varies according to the immediate task or situation. Second, we will discuss some communicative strategies which second language speakers use in order to compensate for gaps in their linguistic knowledge. Third, we will consider how second language learners' speech is received by native speakers.

Although the chapter focusses on second language performance rather than second language development, it is still relevant to the main topic of the book. Throughout the book, we have seen how second language ability develops through communicative use. This means that the nature of this use may contain important clues to the factors which produce learning. Also, since communicative use is the goal as well as a means of learning, better insights into the nature of this goal may point towards more effective ways of helping learners to reach it.

## 7.2 Variability in second language learners' speech

It is well known to teachers that learners are often inconsistent in their performance. In one activity, for example, they may give the impression that they have mastered a particular rule, but a moment later, they may apply it wrongly for no apparent reason. Indeed, teachers are often tempted to reproach learners for their 'carelessness' in failing to make use of what they 'know'.

A number of studies have shown that this kind of variable performance is a normal phenomenon in second language learners' speech. For example, in his study of three Italian children acquiring German, Man-fred Pienemann (1980) found that they did not master an individual rule suddenly, with an abrupt change from using it always wrongly in one interview to using it always correctly in the next. Rather, it was the relative *frequency* of correct and incorrect forms that changed. For example, at one of the interviews, Concetta used the subject-verb inversion rule correctly on 30 per cent of the occasions where the grammar required it. Five weeks later, she used it correctly on 41 per cent of the occasions, and after another four weeks, the proportion had risen to 82 per cent. Similar progressions were taking place in a number of structural domains simultaneously.

Lonna and Wayne Dickerson (L. Dickerson, 1975; L. and W. Dickerson, 1978) found similar variability for learners' pronunciation. They also examined some of the factors which seem to determine which form is used. One such factor appears to be the linguistic environment in which the item occurs. For example, Japanese learners of English came closest to the native pronunciation for /z/ (e.g. as in 'was' or 'reside') when the sound was followed by a vowel. Another factor appears to be the kind of situation or task. For example, when the learners were reading lists of words, they came closest to the target norm. They were further from this norm when reading dialogues and furthest of all from it when they were engaged in free speaking. This pattern of variation is similar to what has frequently been observed in native speakers' use of English: as the task changes from reading word-lists or prose to taking part in free conversation, speakers' pronunciation tends to move further away from the standard norm. The explanation which is usually offered, for both first and second language speakers, is that in free conversation, they pay more attention to the content of their speech and correspondingly less attention to its form. To use a common way of expressing this: in conversation, they 'monitor' their speech less.

We discussed a similar phenomenon briefly in chapter 4 (section 4.2), in connection with the learning of various English morphemes. According to several studies, there is a natural sequence for learning these items. The result is that, at a given stage of proficiency, learners produce them with similar degrees of accuracy in their speech, provided that the purpose of this speech is to communicate meanings. However, when the task is one which requires learners to attend mainly to the form of the language (e.g. in order to carry out manipulative exercises), their speech shows different characteristics. In particular, it contains more target-like forms.

There is evidence from several sources, then, that as learners devote more conscious attention to their speech, they come closer to target norms. This idea forms the basis for Stephen Krashen's 'monitor model' for second language performance. According to this model (which I also mentioned in the previous chapter, section 6.4), second language speakers can monitor their speech by means of linguistic knowledge which they have learnt by conscious means. Speech which is not monitored, on the other hand, comes directly from the system that they have acquired by natural processes. Therefore, monitored speech is more strongly influenced by the correct target norms, while unmonitored speech appears more deviant because it reflects the system which the learner is constructing for himself.

Within this framework, it is the unmonitored, more deviant kind of speech that gives a true picture of the learner's developing competence. Monitoring can increase the superficial accuracy of the speech, provided that:

1  there is sufficient time for monitoring to take place;
2  the learner's attention is focussed on the form of the speech;
3  the relevant rule has been learnt consciously.

However, as Krashen also admits, it is likely that monitoring occurs in varying degrees, rather than being completely present or absent. In addition, we have too little knowledge of the psychological processes involved to be able to state, with any certainty, that only consciously learned rules can be used for monitoring, or that learners' spontaneous output reflects only what they have acquired unconsciously.

Within the skill-learning framework, as I indicated in section 6.4, the more strongly monitored kinds of performance would be those where learners have more time and attentional capacity to use their knowledge for putting together plans which have not become fully automated.

As we have seen in this section, teachers have no cause to feel surprised or discouraged at the apparent inconsistency of their learners, since variability is the rule rather than the exception in second language learners' speech.

## 7.3   Communication strategies

When they are engaged in communication, second language learners often have communicative intentions which they find difficulty in expressing, because of gaps in their linguistic repertoire. If a learner is able to anticipate such a problem, he may be able to forestall it by avoiding communication or modifying what he intended to say. If the problem arises while the learner is already engaged in speaking, he must try to find an alternative way of getting the meaning across. In either case, his way of coping with the situation is what we call his 'communication strategy'.

The main distinguishing characteristic of a communication strategy is that it occurs when a learner becomes aware of a problem with which his current knowledge has difficulty in coping. The speech production process is therefore itself raised to a higher level of consciousness. Similar occasions arise with our native language, when we experience a problem in expressing ourselves and must either change our meaning or grope outside the repertoire of language which comes spontaneously. However, it is unlikely that we can draw a sharp dividing line – in either practical or psychological terms – between speech which is the spontaneous output of a learner's underlying system and speech which is the result of a communication strategy. All language use is a response to some kind of communication problem and a person's awareness of this problem is a matter of varying degree.

In this section, we will look at some of the communication strategies which learners have been observed to use.

### AVOID COMMUNICATING

When learners are already aware of gaps or weaknesses in their repertoire, an obvious strategy is to try to avoid occasions which will present difficulty. For example, many learners find it difficult to present arguments in persuasive ways or to gain the floor when several speakers are competing for turns. They may therefore avoid participating actively in discussions of this nature. As a further example, learners may avoid discussing topics for which they know that they lack the necessary vocabulary.

We have no concrete evidence for relating this or any other communication strategy to personality factors. However, we might speculate that this strategy would be more frequent with learners who dislike risks or uncertainty.

### ADJUST THE MESSAGE

When learners encounter a problem while an exchange is actually taking place, it is usually too late to use avoidance, except by simply abandoning their message half-way through. However, they may decide to alter the meanings which they intended to communicate. For example, they may omit some items of information, make the ideas simpler or less precise, or say something slightly different.

This strategy does not necessarily result in any observable deviation from the conventions of correct language use. It may therefore have particular appeal for learners who are concerned about linguistic accuracy, either because they are being tested or because of their personal desire to conform to native norms.

### USE PARAPHRASE

A learner may use paraphrase – for example, circumlocution or description – in order to express the meaning which he wants to communicate. For example, a learner who did not recall the word for a 'car seat-belt' avoided the need for it by saying *I'd better tie myself in*. A learner who could not recall the word 'kettle' spoke of *the thing that you boil water in*.

Again, this is a suitable strategy for maintaining linguistic accuracy, since it does not necessarily lead to any observable error in the forms used.

USE APPROXIMATION

A learner may decide to use words which express the meaning as closely as possible. This may mean using words which are less specific than the intended meaning (e.g. *some fruit* instead of 'pineapple'). It may also mean using words which really refer to something else but may be interpreted appropriately in the context of the learner's utterance. For example, a learner of French who could not recall the word for a 'shop' spoke instead of *un bureau* (= 'office'). Communication was successful because the topic of the conversation involved buying perfume. However, there are obvious risks involved with this strategy.

The observable language resulting from this strategy may be identical to what we called in chapter 3 (e.g. section 3.2) an 'overgeneralisation error'. Only the learner can know whether, in fact, a conscious communication strategy is involved. Even then, as I indicated earlier in this section, no clear distinction can be made.

CREATE NEW WORDS

A learner may create a new word or phrase, which he hopes will express the desired meaning. The new word may be created by literally translating the elements in a native-language word. For example, a German learner of English who did not know the word for a 'bedside table' coined the word *night-table*, which is a literal translation of the German *Nachttisch*. Alternatively, learners may create words out of second language material, with no apparent influence from the mother tongue. An example in German is *Abwaschmaschine*, created from 'abwaschen' (= 'to wash up') and 'Maschine' (= 'machine') to refer to a 'dishwasher'. In English, an example is *water-holder* (for 'bucket').

There is always a chance, of course, that this strategy will result in a word which actually exists in the second language, especially if (like German) the language has productive rules for word-formation. If an error results, it may again be superficially identical to a type of error mentioned in chapter 3: either a 'transfer error' (c.f. section 3.3) or an 'overgeneralisation error' (c.f. section 3.2).

SWITCH TO THE NATIVE LANGUAGE

Rather than attempt to create a new word with second language material, a speaker may decide to simply lift a word from his own native language.

For example, an English-speaking learner of French produced *Je suis dans la wrong maison* and *un bureau pour cosmetics et perfume.*

Obviously, this strategy is most likely to succeed in situations where the listener has knowledge of the speaker's native language. Classroom learning situations often come into this category. We might also expect learners to resort to this strategy more often when their first and second languages share a significant number of words through common origins or borrowing. The learner may, of course, 'foreignise' the word by making appropriate modifications in pronunciation and morphology.

### USE NON-LINGUISTIC RESOURCES

Even in our native language, we often use non-linguistic resources (e.g. mime, gesture or imitation) to make our meanings clearer. For example, we point and say *Put it there, please,* or we make a gesture and say *It was this kind of shape.* As every learner or teacher knows, second language speakers can profit still more from these non-linguistic means for complementing their linguistic resources.

Although this strategy may be useful at any stage, it is obviously most indispensable when a learner with very little knowledge is compelled to survive in the foreign environment. In this situation, learners are often surprised to discover how much they can achieve by the ingenious and determined linking of words with non-linguistic resources.

### SEEK HELP

Finally, a learner may seek help from outside. This may simply mean using a bilingual dictionary. Alternatively, the speaker may invoke the co-operation of the listener by signalling that he is in difficulty, either directly or by indirect means such as hesitation. Of course, the speaker may simultaneously use another strategy, such as mime or description, in order to indicate the notion that he wishes to express.

These are some of the communication strategies which learners use when they encounter problems in expressing themselves in a second language.

Little is known about the factors that determine which of these strategies a learner decides to use in order to cope with a particular problem. Possible factors which I have already mentioned are the learner's personality or his degree of concern with linguistic accuracy. These probably interact with situational factors, such as the amount of help provided by the non-linguistic context or the likelihood that the listener would understand a native-language word. There seems little doubt that the use of appropriate communication strategies can be regarded as a domain of skill in its own right. A second language learner who is skilled in this domain may communicate more effectively than learners who are considerably more advanced in purely linguistic terms. When we know more about these strategies and their effect, there may be strong arguments for actually training learners in their use.

Another issue about which we have no precise knowledge is the nature of the relationship between communication strategies and learning. Intuitively, we may consider that some of the strategies – such as mime or the use of the native language – are unlikely to produce learning, except in the indirect sense that they enable the interaction to continue and perhaps elicit help from the listener. Other strategies – such as paraphrase or adjusting the message – may not help learners to expand their repertoire, but help them to become more fluent with what they already possess. Other strategies – such as seeking help or creating new words – may lead learners to gain new information about what is appropriate or permissible in the second language.

In view of their importance in enabling communication to take place and the links between communication and learning, the study of communication strategies ought to provide important theoretical and practical insights in the future.

## 7.4   The communicative effect of second language learners' speech

Now that we have looked at the variability of learners' speech and the communication strategies that compensate for weaknesses in their repertoire, we will shift our perspective briefly to the native listener who receives these attempts to communicate. For example, what factors determine whether the listener understands what the learner is trying to say? In what other ways might a native listener evaluate a second language learner's speech?

In most of the relevant studies that have been carried out, native speakers have been presented with samples of speech and asked to interpret it or judge how acceptable it is. The samples have ranged from isolated sentences containing controlled numbers or types of error, to longer extracts from recorded interviews. The picture that emerges is not sufficiently clearly defined for us to draw definite conclusions, but the results suggest that:

1 Errors have less effect on the intelligibility of speech than many second language learners assume. Not surprisingly, however, intelligibility suffers as the number of errors increases.
2 The effect on intelligibility does not depend only on the nature of the error itself. It also depends on how much the wider context (linguistic and non-linguistic) helps the listener to interpret the meaning.

3 Some studies suggest that, on average, vocabulary errors affect communication more than grammatical errors. Pronunciation errors seem to have the least effect, unless they are particularly serious. However, there are obviously more and less serious types of error within each of these three categories.

4 In grammar, 'global' errors generally hinder communication more than 'local' errors. A global error is one which affects the overall organisation of a sentence, such as the wrong use of a conjunction or inappropriate ordering of major word groups. A local error is one whose effect is restricted to the elements within a smaller group, such as the omission of an ending or misuse of the definite article.

5 Learners who use a lot of communication strategies, of the kind discussed in the previous section, are often difficult to understand. Presumably this is not directly a result of the communication strategies, but because the strategies reflect the fact that the learner has special problems in expressing himself.

6 Learners are often difficult to understand if the fluency of their speech is heavily distorted by hesitations, false starts and self-corrections.

7 Independently of their effect on intelligibility, some errors may provoke more negative reactions than others from native speakers. There is some evidence, for example, that errors in verb phrases (e.g. tense marking) tend to be rated as more serious than errors in noun phrases (e.g. use of the article).

8 In general, however, the amount of 'irritation' caused by errors depends mainly on their effect on communication, rather than on some independent scale of seriousness.

9 Native speakers are usually more lenient than non-native language teachers when they are asked to judge the degree of seriousness of errors. Indeed, some errors go completely unnoticed by native evaluators who are not linguists or teachers.

10 There is some evidence (from the study by Dorte Albrechtsen et al., 1980) that native speakers do not form negative judgments about the intelligence and personality of second language learners on the basis of shortcomings in their linguistic or communicative ability.

We may assume that there is considerable variation amongst native listeners in how they perceive second language learners' speech. There is some evidence, for example, that listeners with higher education tend to be more critical of errors than other native speakers. Also, from what we know about attitudes to speech in general, it is likely that listeners' reactions will be affected by how they perceive the speaker's personality or status and how favourably they regard the community to which he belongs. In addition, it is possible that listeners from communities where there are strongly prescriptive attitudes towards language will be particularly critical towards foreigners' attempts to produce their language. These and other possibilities may be clarified by future research.

Studies of the communicative effect of second language learners' speech have obvious potential value in helping us to conceive appropriate goals for learners and suitable criteria for evaluating their performance. At the general level, they emphasise the primacy of intelligibility over formal accuracy. At the more specific level, they indicate some of the linguistic factors which determine whether a learner achieves intelligibility.

## 7.5    Conclusion

In this chapter, we have been concerned with how people perform with a second language, rather than with how they learn it. However, since performance is both the goal of learning and one of the ways in which learning takes place, we have remained close to the main theme of the book.

We have seen that variability is a normal phenomenon as learning progresses and that unexpected errors do not mean that a learner is regressing. We have looked at some of the ways in which communication strategies can compensate for deficiencies in a second language learner's repertoire. Finally, we have discussed the effects of second language learners' speech in communication with native speakers of the language.

# 8 Learning and teaching

## 8.1 Introduction

Research into second language learning has considerably enriched our understanding of the processes that take place and the factors that influence them. However, there are still immense gaps in our knowledge. Many of these have been mentioned in the course of the book. For example: our evidence about natural sequences is limited to only a few aspects of language; our insight into learning strategies such as transfer and generalisation does not extend to explaining why they are applied to some rules but not others; our knowledge of the non-linguistic factors which determine the course of learning is similarly vague and incomplete; and we have practically no understanding at all of the psychological reality and relationships behind such concepts as 'subconscious acquisition' and 'conscious learning'. All of the gaps which I have just mentioned are, of course, in domains which become crucial as soon as we begin to consider possible applications to teaching.

These limitations mean that we should not rush to second language research and demand definitive prescriptions about how we can make learning occur more efficiently. What we can find in this research, however, is a source of insights and ideas about learning which we can add to our present understanding and experience, to help us in our constant search for better ways of teaching. In some cases, these insights and ideas may suggest new orientations and methods. In other cases, they may reinforce developments which have already begun to take place. Always, of course, the final criterion for accepting any pedagogical idea is not whether it is valid from a theoretical perspective, but whether it produces more effective practice.

In the sections which follow, then, I will pick out some of the ideas discussed in this book, and suggest some of the implications that they may have for teaching a second language in the classroom.

## 8.2 Learning occurs both consciously and subconsciously

Perhaps the most important fact that is highlighted by second language research is that progress does not only occur when people make conscious efforts to learn. Progress also occurs as a result of spontaneous, subconscious mechanisms, which are activated when learners are involved in communication with the second language. This insight is not new, of course, but we have come to a new understanding of its importance.

The implications for teaching are far-reaching. In the majority of traditional language-teaching activities, the conscious element is strong: we specify dialogues to be learnt, structures to be practised, words to be memorised, and so on. The subconscious element demands a new range of activities, where learners are focussed not on the language itself, but on the communication of meanings. In these conditions, linguistic competence can develop through the learners' internal processing mechanisms.

In emphasising the need to involve learners in communicative interaction, second language research has reinforced a trend which was already present in language teaching. Teachers' experiences with audio-lingual and audio-visual courses have demonstrated that, on their own, habit-formation techniques are not sufficient to develop the ability to communicate in a language. Learners also need opportunities for communicative use, so that they can integrate separate structures into a creative system for expressing meanings.

From the perspective of recent research, then, communicative interaction provides an opportunity for creative construction to take place in response to the language input. From the skill-learning perspective which is more familiar in teaching, it provides opportunities for whole-task practice (c.f. chapter 6, section 6.3). In either case, communicative interaction provides a situation in which internal processes can create and integrate knowledge, outside the control of the teacher and the consciousness of the learner.

Some teachers and methodologists now take the view that a person's ability to communicate develops almost exclusively through the subconscious aspects of learning ('acquisition' as defined in chapter 6, section 6.4). This belief implies that almost our whole teaching effort should be directed towards creating contexts for language use in the classroom, by means such as listening and reading activities, discussion, communication tasks and role-playing. These contexts should enable learners to construct their own representation of the language, in the same way as they would in a natural environment, and pass through the same sequences of development as a natural learner. Since the learner's attention should be almost entirely on understanding and expressing meanings through language, form-oriented procedures such as conscious drilling or correction should be avoided as much as possible. One approach which tries to implement these principles in the classroom is the 'natural approach' of Tracy Terrell (1977, 1982). Similar principles provide the basis for many attempts to develop second language ability by teaching other material (e.g. history, geography or science) through that language, as in 'immersion programmes' or '*sections bilingues*'.

Teachers and researchers are still involved in exploring to what extent completely 'acquisition-based' approaches, as just described, are feasible and effective in different kinds of learning situation. In the meantime, a more widespread response to the need to provide opportunities for subconscious learning (or whole-task practice) is to include various kinds of communicative activity as one major component within a broader methodological framework. The other major component consists of activities which are 'pre-communicative': that is, they equip learners with some of the sub-skills needed for language use, but do not involve actual communicative interaction. The main framework for teaching is thus as follows:

1 *Pre-communicative activities*. These are a form of part-skill training (c.f. section 6.3). They help learners to master separate aspects of the language, such as sounds or patterns, through either cognitive tech- niques (e.g. explanations, grammar exercises) or habit-forming techniques (e.g. repetition, drills). Learners often focus their conscious attention on the actual items to be learnt.
2 *Communicative activities*. As whole-task practice, these help learners to integrate their separate sub-skills into an effective system for communicating meanings. From a creative construction perspective, they also activate the learners' capacity for acquiring language through natural processes. The learners' attention is focussed on meanings to be communicated rather than on language items to be learnt.

However, there is clearly no strict borderline between these two main categories. We can think of them as representing two halves of a con- tinuum, which extends from the most form-oriented activities at one extreme (e.g. memorising verb-paradigms) to the most meaning-oriented activities at the other (e.g. listening to a gripping story or taking part in an interesting discussion).

## 8.3   Learning can occur without production

The core component of most well-known teaching methodologies con- sists of activities where learners are required to speak or write the second language. The teacher can exercise varying degrees of control over the language that is produced, ranging from repetition at one extreme to free discussion at the other. The underlying assumption is that it is mainly through productive practice that learners internalise the system of the language.

Our observations of natural learning make us question whether productive practice is as central to the basic learning process as we have usually assumed. The evidence suggests that the internal processing mechanisms operate equally effectively (perhaps even more effectively) when the learner is not producing language himself. In the initial stages, for example, there is often a silent period, during which a natural learner produces no language at all. However, he is already constructing a system which will enable him to speak when he is ready. Indeed, the very fact that learners can produce spontaneous utterances which reflect their own created systems is itself evidence that creative construction precedes production, because the utterances could not exist before the system that generates them.

If we accept that creative construction can take place without production, we need to accord a more substantial role to receptive activities than has often been the case. In so doing, we contribute not only to the specific skills of comprehension, but also to the general language competence which underlies all language use. So far as our teaching methodology is concerned, this is a welcome conclusion, because listening and reading activities offer a number of practical advantages in the classroom. For example, they enable us to introduce interesting and motivating materials, relevant to the learners' own concerns; we can devise a wide variety of tasks which provide learners with a clear purpose; and all learners can perform simultaneously, however large the class may be.

The increased importance attached to silent processing as a source of learning is also important for our attitude towards oral activity conducted with the whole class. When a teacher conducts this kind of activity with a class of, say, thirty learners, each individual learner cannot speak, on average, for more than one-thirtieth of the total speaking-time available to members of the class. If the teacher takes up half of the time (e.g. with putting questions and providing correct responses), each learner has an average of thirty seconds speaking-time during a session of half-an-hour. Obviously, if the teacher believes that learning is heavily dependent on the amount of productive use, this situation can present him with a frustrating sense of insufficiency. This feeling is reduced, however, once we accept that learners can develop their competence while they are silent. The crucial factor becomes not so much whether a learner is actually speaking, but whether he is participating in a deeper sense: paying attention to the interaction and processing mentally the language to which he is exposed.

Some teachers and methodologists argue that learners in classrooms, like natural learners, should be allowed to pass through a 'silent period', during which there is no pressure on them to speak the second language at all. During this period, the teacher exposes them to comprehensible input (e.g. language whose meaning is clearly related to visuals or concrete situations) and expects them to respond either non-verbally or in the mother tongue. In this way, learners can lay the foundations for their internal representation of the language, free from the anxiety and distraction that might result from premature demands that they should produce utterances. They are encouraged to speak when they are ready to do so spontaneously, on the basis of their own created system. This procedure is incorporated into the 'natural approach' mentioned in the previous section. The effectiveness of a silent period has also been investigated in empirical studies (e.g. Asher et al., 1974; Postovsky, 1974), with favourable results.

## 8.4 Learners are disposed to follow natural sequences of development

In most language-teaching courses, there is an external syllabus which prescribes the sequence in which language items (especially structural patterns) are to be learnt. Research into second language learning has shown that teachers must also reckon with an *internal* syllabus. This is the sequence in which the learner's internal mechanisms become ready to acquire different items and rules. There may often be conflict between the external and internal syllabuses, with the result that items which are taught are not learnt (also vice versa, if the learner is exposed to language outside the classroom). The most common way in which this conflict becomes evident is through the learner's errors.

In talking about natural sequences, we usually mean one of two things:

1 Learners become ready to acquire item A (e.g. *-s* to mark plural nouns in English) before they are ready to acquire item B (e.g. *-s* to mark third-person verbs).

If we knew enough about this kind of sequence, it might be feasible to modify the teaching syllabus, so that its teaching order would be a direct reflection of the natural learning order. However, we would not expect this to eliminate errors from the learners' speech. This is because, as we saw in chapter 7 (section 7.2), natural acquisition is not a sudden jump into complete mastery, but a process of gradually increasing accuracy.

2 In mastering a particular structural operation (e.g. forming yes/no interrogatives or negatives), natural learning sequences pass through stage X, stage Y, etc.

It is more difficult to envisage this kind of learning sequence being directly reflected in the teaching syllabus, since this would involve teachers in actually presenting their students with the deviant forms produced in the early stages of natural learning. However, knowledge of the natural learning sequence enables us to predict what errors are likely to occur.

We have just seen two possible teaching responses to knowledge about natural learning sequences: when possible, make the teaching sequence reflect the learning sequence, so that they reinforce each other instead of conflicting; when this is not possible, predict a higher proportion of errors, which we can either simply accept as inevitable stages or attempt to eliminate by extra teaching. A third possible response is to abandon the idea of exact structural sequencing, so that the learner's inbuilt syllabus can follow its own preferred path in processing the language. This is the procedure followed in the 'natural' approach mentioned earlier in this chapter. In this approach, any simplification of the language input serves not so much to grade it, as to make it more comprehensible, on the model of the typical adult's speech to young children (see also chapter 5, section 5.4.3).

Apart from any strategic decisions that we may consider adopting in the light of our knowledge about natural sequences, this knowledge can produce changes in the way that errors are treated during classroom interaction. Errors have traditionally been regarded as signs of failure on the part of both the teacher and the learner, and have frequently led to a sense of demoralisation on both sides. Now, however, we realise more clearly that they represent normal stages in the development of communicative skills. We also realise that it is normal for a learner to produce a form correctly in one task but make errors with it in another. We can therefore adopt a less negative stance towards errors. In some activities, for example, a teacher may decide to be selective in the errors which he corrects, e.g. ignoring those which do not relate to previously acquired knowledge. In other activities, he may decide to avoid correcting the forms of the language at all, if this would interfere with the learners' concentration on the communication of meanings. In general, learners can feel less anxiety about producing errors and teachers can respond to them with more tolerance, with beneficial effects on the classroom atmosphere and on the motivation of all concerned.

## 8.5   Communication can take place through a reduced system

Studies of how learners use their second language as a means of communication (c.f. chapter 7) show what a lot can be achieved with an imperfect knowledge of the language system. In part, this merely reinforces the more tolerant attitude towards errors that we discussed in the previous section. In addition, however, it may lead us to consider possible revisions in our overall teaching objectives.

In most language-teaching courses, the objectives are conceived in terms of items to be mastered. A typical syllabus may consist of a graded sequence of structural patterns or an inventory of communicative functions. These items are like building-blocks, from which learners gradually construct a more comprehensive knowledge of the language. The ideal learner would master each item with complete accuracy before moving on to the next.

Our observations of natural learning show that there is an alternative way of conceiving progress. Natural learners do not follow a step-by-step progression through the separate parts of the system. They encompass the whole of the second language from the outset, but reduce it to a simpler system which excludes all but the most basic distinctions. Progress consists in 'filling out' this system with more and more distinctions, so that it becomes more and more refined as a means of communication.

When related to classroom practice, these observations encourage us to conceive our objectives in a similar way: not in terms of individual items which should be mastered to perfection, but in terms of a system which is elaborated globally and increases gradually in communicative potential. Some effects of this might be that:

1 From the earliest stages, we should encourage learners to have confidence in their own system and exploit it for communicative ends. For this, we need a wide repertoire of communicative activities, graded in difficulty (techniques for grading need to be explored).
2 We should encourage learners to compensate for the gaps in their second language knowledge by using communication strategies, even when these may increase the superficial 'foreignness' of their speech. It may eventually become possible to guide them as to the relative effectiveness of different strategies in different situations.
3 In evaluating learners' performance, we should give communicative effectiveness priority over formal accuracy (which does not necessarily mean that we should *abandon* formal accuracy, however). Studies of the communicative effect of second language learners' speech (c.f. chapter 7, section 7.4) may help us to formulate relevant criteria which we can apply in the classroom. We also need to extend our repertoire of techniques for the formal testing of the learner's global communicative system.

The two kinds of progression do not necessarily exclude each other. A teacher may retain a traditional item-by-item syllabus as the main framework of the course but also provide opportunities for global communicative development to occur. This can be carried out within the framework outlined in section 8.2, with pre-communicative activities providing for a step-by-step progression and communicative activities acting as contexts for the global progression.

## 8.6   Learning is affected by complex psychological factors

In seeking to explain why people enjoy different degrees of success in second language learning (given similar opportunities), we were long accustomed to thinking almost exclusively in terms of intelligence and language aptitude. Some people seemed simply to be 'better' at language learning than others. The research of Robert Gardner and Wallace Lambert (1972) made us broaden our view, by demonstrating that attitudes and motivation were equally important. Since then, research and experience have revealed a large number of other psychological factors that might influence the course of learning. Some of these factors were discussed in chapter 5.

Since we understand so little about these factors, we must be careful not to draw premature or unrealistic conclusions for teaching. For example, there may well come a time when we can assess a student's personality or cognitive style and assign him to a suitable teacher or method on the basis of this assessment. However, this time does not seem about to arrive in the near future. In the meantime, we must be content with conclusions of a more general nature. For example:

1   Language learning is a natural response to communicative needs (productive and/or receptive). Therefore, we should try to ensure that learners are always aware of the communicative value of what they are learning. For example, we should help them to relate the language to the social contexts in which it is spoken; we should create communicative contexts in the classroom; learners should be helped to use the language for expressing their own personal needs and their own personality; and when possible, we should arrange contacts with native speakers.

2   In most situations, learning occurs more easily if there are positive attitudes towards the second language community. We should therefore try to break down any prejudices towards this community and help learners to perceive the common interests that link its members with themselves. This may be helped by suitable teaching materials and, again, personal contact with native speakers.

3   For many foreign language learners, their first visit to the foreign country creates a sense of inadequacy and anxiety (so-called 'culture shock'). They need to be prepared for this first contact as thoroughly as possible, with knowledge and coping strategies for everyday situations.

4   In the classroom, anxiety can hinder learning and make learners reluctant to express themselves through the second language. We should therefore avoid becoming over-critical of their performance, try to create space for each learner's individuality to express itself, and work

to produce a relaxed classroom atmosphere with co-operative relationships.

5 Successful learners often adopt certain identifiable learning strategies, such as seeking out practice opportunities or mouthing the answers to questions put to other learners. We can encourage all learners to adopt such strategies.

These five points are intended only as examples, not as a systematic account, of how teaching might be affected by an awareness of psychological factors. Individual teachers will reach other conclusions and decide how they might be implemented. In some cases, this may be through definite procedures (e.g. selecting language relevant to needs or arranging activities which involve co-operation). In other cases, it may be through less tangible modifications of attitude (e.g. to errors) or of emphasis (e.g. on the learners' initiative rather than the teacher's control).

## 8.7 Conclusion

In this final chapter, I have chosen a few of the insights and ideas which result from second language research, and suggested some implications they might have for teaching. I would emphasise again that there can be no question of this research acting as a source of prescriptions about teaching procedures. There are still too many gaps in our knowledge and, in any case, classroom practice must take account of many other variables. Nonetheless, every increase in our knowledge about second language learning should be recognised as having high potential relevance for improving our work in teaching. It is the facilitation of learning, after all, that is the aim and justification for this work.

# Postscript

Research into second language acquisition is a comparatively new field and there are still considerable gaps in our knowledge. For example, we do not yet know much about the development of comprehension skills or about the mastery of pronunciation and vocabulary in a second language. Most crucially for teaching, perhaps, we are still a long way from being able to pinpoint the precise features of the interactions between learners and teachers, or between learners and native speakers, which cause learning to take place most effectively.

However, over the last decade or so, our knowledge has advanced by leaps and bounds. Indeed, so much research has taken place that the writing of this book has posed considerable problems of selection. Obviously, I have had to treat many topics less fully than they deserve and to omit some topics altogether. It is for this reason that I have added a section with detailed suggestions for further reading, which should help the interested reader to continue exploring this fascinating field.

My hope is that I have succeeded in dealing here with aspects of second language learning which not only give a coherent impression of the field, but also show how its discoveries and insights are relevant to our activity in the classroom. There can surely be no doubt that our teaching will benefit – either directly or indirectly – by the deepest possible understanding of the process which lies at the centre of it: learning. As a help towards orientation and a source of practical ideas, second language research has a lot to offer us.

# Further reading

This section gives information about other books and articles which deal with subjects discussed in this book. In selecting the items, I have tried to bear in mind that some readers will want to explore further within general areas, while others will want to follow up specific topics.

Here, I mention only author and date. Precise details of each publication are given in the bibliography.

## General

The books by Brown (1980) and Dulay et al. (1982) provide information about many of the topics mentioned in the present book. Brown includes discussion of the broader educational and psychological background. Dulay et al. discuss a wide range of material mainly from a 'creative construction' perspective. Krashen (1981a and 1982) also considers a wide variety of topics from his own theoretical perspective.

McDonough (1981) includes many topics in his survey of the contributions of psychology to foreign language teaching. Alexander (1979) and Wode (1981) deal with many aspects of second language research in working towards an integrated theory of second language learning.

Some articles which provide useful surveys of research into second language learning are Corder (1975), Hakuta and Cancino (1977), Cook (1978) and Chun (1980).

Many influential papers have been reprinted in volumes edited by Richards (1974), Schumann and Stenson (1975) and Hatch (1978a). Corder (1981) collects together some of his own papers, which have been influential since the late 1960s. Other collections of papers about various aspects of second language learning include Gingras (1978), Richards (1978), Ritchie (1978), Scarcella and Krashen (1980) and Felix (1980).

Readers who are looking for articles about specific aspects of second language learning may find them in journals such as *Language Learning, IRAL, Applied Linguistics, Interlanguage Studies Bulletin* (Utrecht) and *Studies in Second Language Acquisition. TESOL Quarterly, Modern Language Journal, Canadian Modern Language Review* and *English Language Teaching Journal* are among the language-teaching journals which sometimes publish articles about the pedagogical implications of research into second language learning.

## Chapter 1

There are many surveys of research into first language acquisition. The relevant chapters in Clark and Clark (1977) and Slobin (1979) are concise and lucid. Cook (1979) and de Villiers and de Villiers (1979) provide short, accessible accounts. More detail is given by Dale (1976), de Villiers and de Villiers (1978) and Elliot (1981).

## Chapter 2

James (1980) provides a comprehensive account of contrastive analysis, including its psychological assumptions. There are useful chapters in Corder (1973) and Brown (1980). An influential critical assessment of behaviourist principles in foreign language teaching was written by Rivers (1964).

## Chapter 3

Discussion of the results and principles of error analysis can be found in many of the writings of Corder (e.g. 1967, 1971, 1973, 1975, 1978, 1981), who also elaborated many of the concepts mentioned here. Important papers are contained in the collections edited by Svartvik (1973), Richards (1974) and Schumann and Stenson (1975). The relevant chapter in Brown (1980) is useful.

Singleton (1981a) provides an overview and evaluation of conflicting views about the role of transfer. Kellerman (1979), Sharwood Smith (1979) and Sajavaara (1981) analyse transfer from a more theoretical perspective.

## Chapter 4

A general survey and discussion of relevant studies can be found in Hatch (1978b), who also summarises some of the possible criticisms. In Hatch (1978a), several important studies are reprinted. Burt and Dulay (1980), Dulay et al. (1982) and Krashen (1980, 1981a and 1982) summarise relevant findings, with the emphasis on their own research.

## Chapter 5

Surveys of individual and social factors which influence success in second language learning include Burstall (1975), Schumann (1978a) and the relevant chapters in Brown (1980), McDonough (1981), Dulay et al. (1982), Krashen (1982) and Stern (1983).

The studies in Gardner and Lambert (1972) examine the effect of attitude/motivation and aptitude on language proficiency. Other relevant studies include Lukmani (1972), Gardner et al. (1976) and Gardner (1979). Schumann (1976a) tries to define 'social distance' as it affects second language learning. The two British research projects mentioned are reported in Burstall et al. (1974) and Green (1975). The role of English as an 'international' language is discussed in Strevens (1980) and Smith (1981).

Language aptitude tests are described and discussed in Davies (1968) and Ingram (1975). Scovel (1978) discusses research into the effects of anxiety. Clarke (1976) discusses 'culture shock'. A study by Taylor et al. (1977) tries to measure the effect of 'threatened identity' on learning success.

Personality variables are discussed by Guiora et al. (1975), Tucker et al. (1976), Cohen (1977), Naiman et al. (1978), Heyde (1979, summarised in Brown 1980) and Brown (1981). Evidence about age differences is discussed and evaluated by many writers, including Burstall et al. (1974), Burstall (1975), Ervin-Tripp (1974), Schumann (1975a), Stern (1976, 1983), Stern and Weinrib (1977), Genesee (1978) and Singleton (1981b). Krashen (1973) considers the evidence about lateralisation of the brain.

Further references to studies comparing the effectiveness of different methods and techniques can be found in Politzer (1981), Dulay et al. (1982) and Krashen (1982). The nature and importance of the input are discussed by Krashen (e.g. 1980, 1981a and b, 1982), Ellis (1981) and Long (1983).

The active strategies of the successful language learner are analysed by Naiman et al. (1978), Seliger (1977) and Wesche (1979). Other relevant discussions are Rubin (1975, 1981), Stern (1975, 1983) and Cohen (1977).


## Chapter 6

Evidence and discussion relevant to the creative construction model can be found in all the works listed in the bibliography for Corder, for Dulay and Burt, and for Krashen; also in Burt and Dulay (1980) and Dulay et al. (1982).

On the relationship between second language learning, acculturation, and the elaboration of simple codes, see Corder (1975, 1978, 1981), Schumann (1975b, 1976a, 1976b, 1978b, 1978c, 1982), Littlewood (1978), Klein and Dittmar (1979, on the Heidelberg project), Andersen (1980), Stauble (1980) and Meisel et al. (1981).

The skill-learning model is discussed by Levelt (1978). A useful account of the hierarchical nature of speech behaviour can be found in Clark and Clark (1977). The distinction between learning and acquisition is discussed by Krashen (e.g. 1980, 1981a, 1981b, 1982) and Krashen and Terrell (1983). Palmer (1922) proposed a similar distinction. Ideas relevant to integrating learning and acquisition into one model are in Bialystock (1978), Sajavaara (1978), Stevick (1980) and Carroll (1981). An introduction to social learning theory is Bandura (1977).


## Chapter 7

The variability of second language learners' speech is examined and discussed by Dickerson (1975), Dickerson and Dickerson (1978), Tarone (1979), Pienemann (1980), Beebe (1980) and Littlewood (1981a). Krashen's 'monitor model' is described in several places, e.g. Krashen (1980, 1981a, 1982); for a critique and defence, see McLaughlin (1978) and Krashen (1979).

Studies of learners' communication strategies are reported and discussed in Tarone (1977, 1980), Corder (1978, 1981), Faerch and Kasper (1980, 1983) and Bialystock and Fröhlich (1980). Littlewood (1979) analyses communicative performance in a second language.

Ludwig (1982) provides an overview of recent studies of the communicative effect of learners' speech. 'Global' and 'local' errors are discussed by Burt and Kiparsky (1975). James (1977) discusses the judgment of error gravity.

## Chapter 8

Many of the books and articles mentioned under previous chapters include some discussion of how the conclusions might affect teaching.

Some works which give special prominence to the implications of research into second language acquisition for teaching are Frith (1978), several papers in Gingras (1978), Krashen (1980, 1981b, 1982), Burt and Dulay (1981), Ellis (1981), Gadalla (1981), McDonough (1981) and Ludwig (1982). Tarone et al. (1976) and Hatch (1979) warn against applying results too hastily.

The methodological framework outlined in section 8.2 is the basis for Littlewood (1981b), where its practical implications are discussed further. The 'natural approach' is described in Terrell (1977, 1982) and Krashen and Terrell (1983). The incorporation of a silent period into classroom learning is discussed by Asher et al. (1974), Postovsky (1974) and Krashen (as above). Blair (1983) includes papers on the natural approach and the silent period. The importance of the psychological and interpersonal climate in the classroom is discussed in many places, e.g. Stevick (1980) and other papers in Blair (1983).

## Postscript

Exploratory studies of interaction between learners and teachers can be found in Allwright (1975), Chaudron (1977) and Fanselow (1977). Hatch (1978c) and Long (1983) report on studies of interaction between learners and native speakers. Larsen-Freeman (1980) contains several papers which deal with the application of 'discourse analysis' in second language research.

# Bibliography

Adams, M. A. 1978. 'Methodology for examining second language acquisition'.
In Hatch, 1978a

Alatis, J. E., H. B. Altman and P. M. Alatis (eds.). 1981. *The Second Language
Classroom: Directions for the 1980s*. Oxford University Press

Albrechtsen, D., B. Henriksen and C. Faerch. 1980. 'Native speakers' reactions to
learners' spoken interlanguage'. *Language Learning* vol. 30, no. 2, pp. 365–96

Alexander, R. 1979. *Elements of a Theory of Second Language Learning*.
Frankfurt-am-Main: Peter Lang

Allwright, R. L. 1975. 'Problems in the study of teachers' treatment of learner
error'. In M. K. Burt and H. C. Dulay (eds.) *On TESOL '75*. Washington D.C.:
TESOL

Andersen, R. W. 1980. 'The role of creolization in Schumann's pidginization
hypothesis for second language learning'. In Scarcella and Krashen, 1980

Asher, J. J., J. A. Kusudo and R. De La Torre. 1974. 'Learning a second language
through commands: the second field test'. *Modern Language Journal* vol. 58,
nos. 1–2, pp. 24–32

Bailey, N., C. Madden and S. Krashen. 1974. 'Is there a "natural sequence" in
adult second language learning?' *Language Learning* vol. 24, no. 2, pp.
235–43. Reprinted in Hatch, 1978a

Bandura, A. 1977. *Social Learning Theory*. New Jersey: Prentice Hall

Beebe, L. M. 1980. 'Sociolinguistic variation and style shifting in second
language acquisition'. *Language Learning* vol. 30, no. 2, pp. 433–47

Bellugi-Klima, U. 1968. 'Linguistic mechanisms underlying child speech'. In E.
M. Zale (ed.) *Proceedings of the Conference on Language and Language
Behavior*. New York: Appleton-Century-Crofts

Bialystock, E. 1978. 'A theoretical model of second language learning'. *Language
Learning* vol. 28, no. 1, pp. 69–83

Bialystock, E. and M. Fröhlich. 1980. 'Oral communication strategies for lexical
difficulties'. *Interlanguage Studies Bulletin* (Utrecht) vol. 5, no. 1, pp. 3–29

Blair, R. W. (ed.). 1983. *Innovative Approaches to Language Teaching*. Rowley,
Mass.: Newbury House

Bloom, L. M. 1970. *Language Development: Form and Function in Emerging
Grammars*. Cambridge, Mass.: MIT Press

Brown, H. D. 1980. *Principles of Language Learning and Teaching*. New Jersey:
Prentice Hall

Brown, H. D. 1981. 'Affective factors in second language learning'. In Alatis et
al., 1981

Brown, R. 1973. *A First Language: The Early Stages*. Harmondsworth: Penguin
Books

Burstall, C. 1975. 'Factors affecting foreign-language learning: a consideration of some recent findings'. *Language Teaching and Linguistics: Abstracts* vol. 8, no. 1, pp. 5–25. Reprinted in Kinsella, 1978

Burstall, C., M. Jamieson, S. Cohen and M. Hargreaves. 1974. *Primary French in the Balance*. Slough: NFER

Burt, M. K. and H. C. Dulay. 1980. 'On acquisition orders'. In Felix, 1980

Burt, M. K. and H. C. Dulay. 1981. 'Optimal language learning environments'. In Alatis et al., 1981

Burt, M. K. and C. Kiparsky. 1975. 'Global and local mistakes'. In Schumann and Stenson, 1975

Butterworth, G. and E. Hatch. 1978. 'A Spanish-speaking adolescent's acquisition of English syntax'. In Hatch, 1978a

Cancino, H., E. J. Rosansky and J. H. Schumann. 1978. 'The acquisition of English negatives and interrogatives by native Spanish speakers'. In Hatch, 1978a

Carroll, J. B. 1981. 'Conscious and automatic processes in language learning'. *Canadian Modern Language Review* vol. 37, no. 3, pp. 462–74

Carroll, J. B. and S. Sapon. 1959. *Modern Language Aptitude Test*. New York: Psychological Corporation

Chaudron, C. 1977. 'A descriptive model of discourse in the corrective treatment of learners' errors'. *Language Learning* vol. 27, no. 1, pp. 29–46

Chun, J. 1980. 'A survey of research in second language acquisition'. *Modern Language Journal* vol. 64, no. 3, pp. 287–96

Clark, H. H. and E. V. Clark. 1977. *Psychology and Language*. New York: Harcourt Brace Jovanovich

Clarke, M. A. 1976. 'Second language acquisition as a clash of consciousness'. *Language Learning* vol. 26, no. 2, pp. 377–90

Cohen, A. 1977. 'Successful second-language speakers: a review of the literature'. *Balshanut Shimushit* no. 1, pp. 3–21

Cook, V. J. 1978. 'Second-language learning: a psycholinguistic perspective'. *Language Teaching and Linguistics: Abstracts* vol. 11, no. 2, pp. 73–89. Reprinted in Kinsella, 1983

Cook, V. J. 1979. *Young Children and Language*. London: Edward Arnold

Corder, S. P. 1967. 'The significance of learners' errors'. *IRAL* vol. 5, no. 4, pp. 161–70. Reprinted in Richards, 1974; Schumann and Stenson, 1975; and Corder, 1981

Corder, S. P. 1971. 'Idiosyncratic dialects and error analysis'. *IRAL* vol. 9, no. 2, pp. 147–60. Reprinted in Richards, 1974; Schumann and Stenson, 1975; and Corder, 1981

Corder, S. P. 1973. *Introducing Applied Linguistics*. Harmondsworth: Penguin Books

Corder, S. P. 1975. 'Error analysis, interlanguage and second language acquisition'. *Language Teaching and Linguistics: Abstracts* vol. 8, no. 4, pp. 201–18. Reprinted in Kinsella, 1978

Corder, S. P. 1978. 'Language-learner language'. In Richards, 1978

Corder, S. P. 1981. *Error Analysis and Interlanguage*. Oxford University Press

Cromer, R. F. 1974. 'The development of language and cognition: the cognition hypothesis'. In B. Foss (ed.) *New Perspectives in Child Development*. Harmondsworth: Penguin Books

# Bibliography

Dale, P.S. 1976. *Language Development: Structure and Function*, second edition.New York: Holt, Rinehart & Winston

Davies, A. (ed.). 1968. *Language Testing Symposium*. Oxford University Press

de Villiers, J. G. and P. A. de Villiers. 1973. 'A cross-sectional study of the acquisition of grammatical morphemes in child speech'. *Journal of Psycholinguistic Research* vol. 2, no. 3, pp. 267–78

de Villiers, J. G. and P. A. de Villiers. 1978. *Language Acquisition*. Cambridge, Mass.: Harvard University Press

de Villiers, P. A. and J. G. de Villiers. 1979. *Early Language*. London: Fontana and Open Books

Dickerson, L. J. 1975. 'The learner's interlanguage as a system of variable rules'. *TESOL Quarterly* vol. 9, no. 4, pp. 401–7

Dickerson, L. J. and W. B. Dickerson. 1978. 'Learning to pronounce: research responses to classroom concerns'. *English Teaching Forum* vol. 16, no. 4, pp. 13–15

Dulay, H. C. and M. K. Burt. 1973. 'Should we teach children syntax?' *Language Learning* vol. 23, no. 2, pp. 245–57

Dulay, H. C. and M. K. Burt. 1974a. 'You can't learn without goofing: an analysis of children's second language errors'. In Richards, 1974

Dulay, H. C. and M. K. Burt. 1974b. 'Natural sequences in child second language acquisition'. *Language Learning* vol. 24, no. 1, pp. 37–53. Reprinted in Hatch, 1978a

Dulay, H. C. and M. K. Burt. 1974c. 'A new perspective on the creative construction processes in child second language acquisition'. *Language Learning* vol. 24, no. 2, pp. 253–78

Dulay, H. C., M. K. Burt and S. D. Krashen. 1982. *Language Two*. Oxford University Press

Elliot, A. J. 1981. *Child Language*. Cambridge University Press

Ellis, R. 1981. 'The role of input in language acquisition: some implications for second language teaching'. *Applied Linguistics* vol. 2, no. 1, pp. 70–82

Ervin-Tripp, S. M. 1974. 'Is second language learning like the first?' *TESOL Quarterly* vol. 8, no. 2, pp. 111–27. Reprinted in Hatch, 1978a

Ervin-Tripp, S. M. 1977. 'Wait for me, roller skate!' In Ervin-Tripp and Mitchell-Kernan, 1977

Ervin-Tripp, S. M. and C. Mitchell-Kernan (eds.). 1977. *Child Discourse*. New York: Academic Press

Faerch, C. and G. Kasper. 1980. 'Processes and strategies in foreign language learning and communication'. *Interlanguage Studies Bulletin* (Utrecht) vol. 5, no. 1, pp. 47–118

Faerch, C. and G. Kasper (eds.). 1983. *Strategies in Interlanguage Communication*. London: Longman

Fanselow, J. F. 1977. 'Beyond Rashomon: conceptualizing and describing the teaching act.' *TESOL Quarterly* vol. 11, no. 1, pp. 17–39

Fathman, A. 1975. 'The relationship between age and second language productive ability'. *Language Learning* vol. 25, no. 2, pp. 245–54

Fathman, A. 1979. 'The value of morpheme order studies for second language learning'. *Working Papers in Bilingualism* (Toronto) no. 18, pp. 180–99

Felix, S. W. (ed.). 1980. *Second Language Development: Trends and Issues.* Tübingen: Gunter Narr

Felix, S. W. 1981. 'The effect of formal instruction on second language acquisition'. *Language Learning* vol. 31, no. 1, pp. 87–112

Frith, M. B. 1978. 'Interlanguage theory: implications for the classroom'. *McGill Journal of Education* vol. 8, no. 2, pp. 155–65

Gadalla, B. J. 1981. 'Language acquisition research and the language teacher'. *Studies in Second Language Acquisition* vol. 4, no. 1, pp. 60–9

Gardner, R. C. 1979. 'Social psychological aspects of second language acquisition'. In H. Giles and R. St. Clair (eds.) *Language and Social Psychology.* Oxford: Blackwell

Gardner, R. C. 1980. 'On the validity of affective variables in second language acquisition: conceptual, contextual and statistical considerations'. *Language Learning* vol. 30, no. 2, pp. 255–70

Gardner, R. C. and W. Lambert. 1972. *Attitudes and Motivation in Second Language Learning.* Rowley, Mass.: Newbury House

Gardner, R. C., P. C. Smythe, R. Clément and L. Gliksman. 1976. 'Second language learning: a social psychological perspective'. *Canadian Modern Language Review* vol. 32, no. 3, pp. 198–213

Genesee, F. 1976. 'The role of intelligence in second language learning'. *Language Learning* vol. 26, no. 2, pp. 267–80

Genesee, F. 1978. 'Is there an optimal age for starting second language instruction?' *McGill Journal of Education* vol. 13, no. 2, pp. 145–54

Gingras, R. C. (ed.). 1978. *Second Language Acquisition and Foreign Language Teaching.* Washington, D.C.: Center for Applied Linguistics

Green, P. S. (ed.). 1975. *The Language Laboratory in School.* Edinburgh: Oliver & Boyd

Guiora, A. Z., M. Paluszny, B. Beit-Hallahmi, J. C. Catford, R. E. Cooley and Y. C. Dull. 1975. 'Language and person: studies in language behaviour'. *Language Learning* vol. 25, no. 1, pp. 43–61

Hakuta, K. 1974a. 'A report on the development of grammatical morphemes in a Japanese girl learning English as a second language'. *Working Papers in Bilingualism* (Toronto) no. 3, pp. 18–44. Reprinted in Hatch, 1978a

Hakuta, K. 1974b. 'Prefabricated patterns and the emergence of structure in second language acquisition'. *Language Learning* vol. 24, no. 2, pp. 287–97

Hakuta, K. 1976. 'Becoming bilingual: a case study of a Japanese child learning English'. *Language Learning* vol. 26, no. 2, pp. 321–51

Hakuta, K. and H. Cancino. 1977. 'Trends in second-language-acquisition research'. *Harvard Educational Review* vol. 47, no. 3, pp. 295–326

Halliday, M. A. K. 1975. *Learning How to Mean.* London: Edward Arnold

Hatch, E. M. (ed.). 1978a. *Second Language Acquisition: A Book of Readings.* Rowley, Mass.: Newbury House

Hatch, E. M. 1978b. 'Acquisition of syntax in a second language'. In Richards, 1978

Hatch, E. M. 1978c. 'Discourse analysis and second language acquisition'. In Hatch, 1978a

Hatch, E. M. 1979. 'Apply with caution'. *Studies in Second Language Acquisition* vol. 2, no. 1, pp. 123–43

# Bibliography

Heyde, A. 1979. *The Relationship between Self-Esteem and the Oral Production of a Second Language*. Ph.D. Thesis, University of Michigan. Discussed in Brown, 1980

Huang, J. and E. M. Hatch. 1978. 'A Chinese child's acquisition of English'. In Hatch, 1978a

Ingram, E. 1975. 'Psychology and language learning'. In J. P. B. Allen and S. P. Corder (eds.). *Papers in Applied Linguistics* (= Edinburgh Course in Applied Linguistics vol. 2). Oxford University Press

Jain, M. P. 1974. 'Error analysis: source, cause and significance'. In Richards, 1974

James, C. 1977. 'Judgments of error gravities'. *English Language Teaching Journal* vol. 31, no. 2, pp. 116–24

James, C. 1980. *Contrastive Analysis*. London: Longman

Kellerman, E. 1979. 'Transfer and non-transfer: where we are now'. *Studies in Second Language Acquisition* vol. 2, no. 1, pp. 37–57

Kinsella, V. (ed.). 1978. *Language Teaching and Linguistics: Surveys*. Cambridge University Press

Kinsella, V. (ed.). 1983. *Cambridge Language Teaching Surveys 1*. Cambridge University Press

Klein, W. and N. Dittmar. 1979. *Developing Grammars: The Acquisition of Syntax by Foreign Workers*. Berlin: Springer

Krashen, S. D. 1973. 'Lateralisation, language learning and the critical period: some new evidence'. *Language Learning* vol. 23, no. 1, pp. 63–74

Krashen, S. D. 1979. 'A response to McLaughlin, "The Monitor Model: some methodological considerations"'. *Language Learning* vol. 29, no. 1, pp. 151–67

Krashen, S. D. 1980. 'Relating theory and practice in adult second language acquisition'. In Felix, 1980

Krashen, S. D. 1981a. *Second Language Acquisition and Second Language Learning*. Oxford: Pergamon

Krashen, S. D. 1981b. 'Effective second language acquisition: insights from research'. In Alatis et al., 1981

Krashen, S. D. 1982. *Principles and Practice in Second Language Acquisition*. Oxford: Pergamon

Krashen, S. D., J. Butler, R. Birnbaum and J. Robertson. 1978. 'Two studies in language acquisition and language learning'. *ITL: Review of Applied Linguistics* nos. 39–40, pp. 73–92

Krashen, S. D. and T. D. Terrell. 1983. *The Natural Approach: Language Acquisition in the Classroom*. Oxford: Pergamon

Lado, R. 1957. *Linguistics Across Cultures*. Ann Arbor: University of Michigan Press

Larsen-Freeman, D. E. 1975. 'The acquisition of grammatical morphemes by adult ESL students'. *TESOL Quarterly* vol. 9, no. 4, pp. 409–20

Larsen-Freeman, D. E. 1976. 'An explanation for the morpheme accuracy order of learners of English as a second language'. *Language Learning* vol. 26, no. 1, pp. 125–35. Reprinted in Hatch, 1978a

Larsen-Freeman, D. E. (ed.). 1980. *Discourse Analysis in Second Language Acquisition*. Rowley, Mass.: Newbury House

Levelt, W. J. M. 1978. 'Skill theory and language teaching'. *Studies in Second Language Acquisition* vol. 1, no. 1, pp. 53–70

Levin, L. 1972. *Comparative Studies in Foreign Language Teaching*. Stockholm: Almqvist & Wiksell

Littlewood, W. T. 1978. 'The transmission of functional and social information in learners' speech'. In G. Nickel (ed.). *Sociolinguistics*. Stuttgart: Hochschulverlag

Littlewood, W. T. 1979. 'Communicative performance in language-developmental contexts'. *IRAL* vol. 17, no. 2, pp. 123–38

Littlewood, W. T. 1981a. 'Language variation and second language acquisition theory'. *Applied Linguistics* vol. 2, no. 2, pp. 150–8

Littlewood, W. T. 1981b. *Communicative Language Teaching: An Introduction*. Cambridge University Press

Long, M. H. 1980. 'Inside the "black box": methodological issues in classroom research on language learning'. *Language Learning* vol. 30, no. 1, pp. 1–42

Long, M. H. 1983. 'Native speaker/non-native speaker conversation and the negotiation of comprehensible input'. *Applied Linguistics* vol. 4, no. 2, pp. 126–41

Ludwig, J. 1982. 'Native-speaker judgments of second language learners' efforts at communication: a review'. *Modern Language Journal* vol. 66, no. 3, 274–83

Lukmani, Y. 1972. 'Motivation to learn and language proficiency'. *Language Learning* vol. 22, no. 2, pp. 261–73

McDonough, S. H. 1981. *Psychology in Foreign Language Teaching*. London: Allen & Unwin

McLaughlin, B. 1978. 'The Monitor Model: some methodological considerations'. *Language Learning* vol. 28, no. 2, pp. 309–32

Meisel, J. M. 1980. 'Linguistic simplification: a study of immigrant workers' speech and foreigner talk'. In Felix, 1980

Meisel, J. M., H. Clahsen and M. Pienemann. 1981. 'On determining developmental stages in natural second language acquisition'. *Studies in Second Language Acquisition* vol. 3, no. 2, pp. 109–35

Mitchell-Kernan, C. and K. T. Kernan. 1977. 'Pragmatics of directive choice among children'. In Ervin-Tripp and Mitchell-Kernan, 1977

Naiman, N. M., M. Fröhlich and H. H. Stern. 1978. *The Good Language Learner*. Toronto: Ontario Institute for Studies in Education

Nemser, W. 1971. 'Approximative systems for foreign language learners'. *IRAL* vol. 9, no. 2, pp. 219–27. Reprinted in Richards, 1974

Palmer, H. E. 1922. *The Principles of Language-Study*. Reprinted by Oxford University Press, 1964

Pienemann, M. 1980. 'The second language acquisition of immigrant children'. In Felix, 1980

Pimsleur, P. 1968. *Language Aptitude Battery*. New York: Harcourt Brace & World

Politzer, R. L. 1981. 'Effective language teaching: insights from research'. In Alatis et al., 1981

Porter, J. H. 1977. 'A cross-sectional study of morpheme acquisition in first language learners'. *Language Learning* vol. 27, no. 1, pp. 47–62

Postovsky, V. A. 1974. 'Effects of delay in oral practice at the beginning of second language learning'. *Modern Language Journal* vol. 58, nos. 5–6, pp. 229–39

Ramsey, C. and E. Wright. 1974. 'Age and second language learning'. *Journal of Social Psychology* vol. 94, pp. 115–21

Ravem, R. 1968. 'Language acquisition in a second language environment'. *IRAL* vol. 6, no. 2, pp. 175–85. Reprinted in Richards, 1974

Ravem, R. 1978. 'Two Norwegian children's acquisition of English syntax'. In Hatch, 1978a

Richards, J. C. 1971. 'A non-contrastive approach to error analysis'. *English Language Teaching* vol. 25, no. 3, pp. 204–19. Reprinted in Richards, 1974

Richards, J. C. (ed.). 1974. *Error Analysis: Perspectives on Second Language Acquisition*. London: Longman

Richards, J. C. (ed.). 1978. *Understanding Second and Foreign Language Learning: Issues and Approaches*. Rowley, Mass.: Newbury House

Ritchie, W. C. (ed.). 1978. *Second Language Acquisition Research: Issues and Implications*. New York: Academic Press

Rivers, W. M. 1964. *The Psychologist and the Foreign Language Teacher*. University of Chicago Press

Rosansky, E. 1976. 'Methods and morphemes in second language acquisition research'. *Language Learning* vol. 26, no. 2, pp. 409–25

Rubin, J. 1975. 'What the "good language learner" can teach us'. *TESOL Quarterly* vol. 9, no. 1, pp. 41–51

Rubin, J. 1981. 'Study of cognitive processes in second language learning'. *Applied Linguistics* vol. 2, no. 2, pp. 117–31

Sajavaara, K. 1978. 'The monitor model and monitoring in foreign language speech communication'. In Gingras, 1978

Sajavaara, K. 1981. 'The nature of first language transfer: English as L2 in a foreign language setting'. Department of English, University of Jyväskylä

Scarcella, R. and S. D. Krashen (eds.). 1980. *Research in Second Language Acquisition*. Rowley, Mass.: Newbury House

Schumann, J. H. 1975a. 'Affective factors and the problem of age in second language acquisition'. *Language Learning* vol. 25, no. 2, pp. 209–35

Schumann, J. H. 1975b. 'Implications of pidginization and creolization for the study of adult second language acquisition. In Schumann and Stenson, 1975

Schumann, J. H. 1976a. 'Social distance as a factor in second language acquisition'. *Language Learning* vol. 26, no. 1, pp. 135–43

Schumann, J. H. 1976b. 'Second language acquisition: the pidginization hypothesis'. *Language Learning* vol. 26, no. 2, pp. 391–408. Reprinted in Hatch, 1978a

Schumann, J. H. 1978a. 'Social and psychological factors in second language acquisition'. In Richards, 1978

Schumann, J. H. 1978b. 'The acculturation model for second language learning'. In Gingras, 1978

Schumann, J. H. 1978c. 'The relationship of pidginization, creolization and decreolization to second language acquisition'. *Language Learning* vol. 28, no. 2, pp. 367–79

Schumann, J. H. 1982. 'Simplification, transfer and relexification as aspects of pidginization and early second language acquisition'. *Language Learning* vol. 32, no. 2, pp. 337–66

Schumann, J. H. and N. Stenson (eds.). 1975. *New Frontiers in Second Language Learning*. Rowley, Mass.: Newbury House

Scovel, T. 1978. 'The effect of affect on foreign language learning: a review of the anxiety research'. *Language Learning* vol. 28, no. 1, pp. 129–42

Seliger, H. W. 1977. 'Does practice make perfect?: a study of interaction patterns and L2 competence'. *Language Learning* vol. 27, no. 2, pp. 263–78

Selinker, L. 1972. 'Interlanguage'. *IRAL* vol. 10, no. 3, pp. 201–31. Reprinted in Richards, 1974, and in Schumann and Stenson, 1975

Selinker, L., M. Swain and G. Dumas. 1975. 'The interlanguage hypothesis extended to children'. *Language Learning* vol. 25, no. 1, pp. 139–52

Sharwood Smith, M. 1979. 'Strategies, language transfer and the simulation of the second language learner's mental operations'. *Language Learning* vol. 29, no. 2, pp. 345–61

Singleton, D. M. 1981a. 'Language transfer: a review of some recent research'. Occasional Paper no. 1, Centre for Language and Communication Studies, Trinity College, Dublin

Singleton, D. M. 1981b. 'Age as a factor in second language acquisition'. Occasional Paper no. 3, Centre for Language and Communication Studies, Trinity College, Dublin

Skinner, B. F. 1957. *Verbal Behavior*. New York: Appleton-Century-Crofts

Slobin, D. I. 1973. 'Cognitive prerequisites for the development of grammar'. In C. Ferguson and D. I. Slobin (eds.) *Studies of Child Language Development*. New York: Holt, Rinehart & Winston

Slobin, D. I. 1979. *Psycholinguistics*, second edition. Glenview: Scott, Foresman

Smith, L. E. (ed.). 1981. *English for Cross-Cultural Communication*. London: MacMillan

Snow, C. and M. Hoefnagel-Höhle. 1978. 'Age differences in second language acquisition'. In Hatch, 1978a

Stauble, A. E. 1980. 'Acculturation and second language acquisition'. In Scarcella and Krashen, 1980

Stern, H. H. 1975. 'What can we learn from the good language learner?' *Canadian Modern Language Review* vol. 31, no. 4, pp. 304–18

Stern, H. H. 1976. 'Optimal age: myth or reality?' *Canadian Modern Language Review* vol. 32, no. 3, pp. 283–94

Stern, H. H. 1983. *Fundamental Concepts in Language Teaching*. Oxford University Press

Stern, H. H. and A. Weinrib. 1977. 'Foreign languages for younger children: trends and assessment'. *Language Teaching and Linguistics: Abstracts* vol. 10, no. 1, pp. 5–25. Reprinted in Kinsella, 1978

Stevick, E. W. 1980. *Teaching Languages: A Way and Ways*. Rowley, Mass.: Newbury House

Stockwell, R., J. D. Bowen and J. W. Martin. 1965. *The Grammatical Structures of English and Spanish*. University of Chicago Press

Strevens, P. 1980. *Teaching English as an International Language*. Oxford: Pergamon

Svartvik, J. 1973. *Errata: Papers in Error Analysis*. Lund: Gleerup

# Bibliography

Tarone, E. 1977. 'Conscious communication strategies in interlanguage: a progress report'. In H. D. Brown, C. Yorio and R. Crymes (eds.) *On TESOL '77*. Washington D. C.: TESOL

Tarone, E. 1979. 'Interlanguage as chameleon'. *Language Learning* vol. 29, no. 1, pp. 181–91

Tarone, E. 1980. 'Communication strategies, foreigner talk, and repair in interlanguage'. *Language Learning* vol. 30, no. 2, pp. 417–31

Tarone, E. 1983. 'On the variability of interlanguage systems'. *Applied Linguistics* vol. 4, no. 2, pp. 142–63

Tarone, E., M. Swain and A. Fathman. 1976. 'Some limitations to the classroom applications of current second language acquisition research'. *TESOL Quarterly* vol. 10, no. 1, pp. 19–32

Taylor, B. 1975. 'The use of overgeneralization and transfer learning strategies by elementary and intermediate students in ESL'. *Language Learning* vol. 25, no. 1, pp. 73–107

Taylor, D. M., R. Meynard and E. Rheault. 1977. 'Threat to ethnic identity and second language learning'. In H. Giles (ed.) *Language, Ethnicity and Intergroup Relations*. London: Academic Press

Terrell, T. D. 1977. 'A natural approach to second language acquisition and learning'. *Modern Language Journal* vol. 61, no. 7, pp. 325–37

Terrell, T. D. 1982. 'The natural approach to language teaching: an update'. *Modern Language Journal* vol. 66, no. 2, pp. 121–32

Tucker, G. R., E. Hamayan and F. H. Genesee. 1976. 'Affective, cognitive and social factors in second language acquisition'. *Canadian Modern Language Review* vol. 32, no. 3, pp. 214–26

Upshur, J. 1968. 'Four experiments on the relation between foreign language teaching and learning'. *Language Learning* vol. 18, nos. 1–2, pp. 111–24

Wagner-Gough, J. 1978. 'Excerpts from comparative studies in second language learning'. In Hatch, 1978a

Wardhaugh, R. 1970. 'The contrastive analysis hypothesis'. *TESOL Quarterly* vol. 4, no. 2, pp. 123–30. Reprinted in Schumann and Stenson, 1975

Wesche, M. B. 1979. 'Learning behaviors of successful adult students on intensive training'. *Canadian Modern Language Review* vol. 35, no. 3, pp. 415–30

Whitman, R. L. and K. L. Jackson. 1972. 'The unpredictability of contrastive analysis'. *Language Learning* vol. 22, no. 1, pp. 29–41

Wode, H. 1976. 'Developmental sequences in naturalistic L2 acquisition'. *Working Papers in Bilingualism* (Toronto) no. 11, pp. 1–31. Reprinted in Hatch, 1978a

Wode, H. 1981. *Learning a Second Language: An Integrated View of Language Acquisition*. Tübingen: Gunter Narr

Wong-Fillmore, L. 1976. 'The second time around: cognitive and social strategies in second language acquisition'. Ph.D. Thesis, Stanford University. Discussed in Hakuta and Cancino, 1977; summary in Hatch, 1978a

# Index

## Index

internal syllabus
   defined, 34–5
   evidence for, 36–50
   in the classroom, 94–5
   *see also* creative construction,
      learning processes
interrogatives
   in first language learning, 12
   in second language learning, 44–5

learning
   as distinct from acquisition, 3, 66,
      76–7, 90–2
   reasons for studying, 1–2
learning processes, 29–30, 35, 49–50
   *see also* creative construction,
      internal syllabus
longitudinal studies, 10

methodology for teaching, 90–4
models of learning, 69–80
monitor theory, 38, 77, 82–3
morpheme sequences
   in first language learning, 9–11
   in second language learning, 37–41
motivation, 53–7, 63
   *see also* acculturation hypothesis

natural learning sequences, *see*
      creative construction, internal
      syllabus
negatives
   in first language learning, 11–12
   in second language learning, 41–4

objectives in teaching, 95–6
opportunities for learning, 57–62
overgeneralisation
   defined, 23–4
   in a skill-learning model, 75
   in first language learning, 14
   in second language learning, 23–5,
      27–8
   *see also* learning processes

performance
   errors of, 31–2
   in a second language, 81–9
   *see also* competence

personality, 64–5
pre-fabricated patterns, 47–9
productive practice, 70, 73–5, 92–4
psychological factors
   effects on learning, 52–7, 62–6
   in the classroom, 97–8

reduced system
   by omission, 28–9
   communication with, 95–6
routine formulas, 47–9

second vs. foreign language, 2, 54
self-esteem, 64
silent period, 92–4
simple codes hypothesis, 71–3
simplification, 28–9
   *see also* learning processses
skill learning
   as a model for second language
      learning, 73–6
   reconciled with creative
      construction, 76–80
social learning, 78–9

teaching
   effects on learning, 60–2
   errors caused by, 32–3
   implications of research for, 90–8
   relevance of developmental studies
      for, 36–7
telegraphic speech, 7–9
   *see also* affirmatives
tolerance for ambiguity, 64
transfer
   as a learning process, 25–7, 40, 42,
      45, 49, 73
   behaviourist view of, 17–18, 21
   in a skill-learning model, 75
   *see also* learning processes
transitional competence, 33

variation
   between learners, 40–1, 42–3, 45,
      46, 49
   causes of, 51–68
   difficulties in studying, 52–3
   in a learner's performance, 38, 81–3